YURY TRIFONOV

A CRITICAL STUDY

Nina Kolesnikoff

Ardis, Ann Arbor

The present study was written during my sabbatical leave in 1984-85. I am grateful to McMaster University both for granting me leave and for the financial support that enabled me to publish this book.

Parts of the book first appeared in *The Russian Language Journal*, no. 118 (1980) and no. 140 (1987). I am grateful to the editors for permission to reprint them.

N.K.

Ardis Publishers
2901 Heatherway
Ann Arbor, Michigan 48104

Library of Congress Cataloging-in-Publication Data

Kolesnikoff, Nina, 1943–
Yuri Trifonov : a critical study / by Nina Kolesnikoff.
p. cm.
Includes bibliographical references.
ISBN 0-87501-051-2 (alk. paper)
1. Trifonov, IUrii Valentinovich, 1925—Criticism and
interpretation. I. Title.
PG3489.R5Z75 1990
891.73'44—dc20   90-35870
CIP

1000538555

CONTENTS

INTRODUCTION

When Yury Trifonov died suddenly in 1981 at the age of fifty-five, he left behind six novels, four novellas and several collections of short stories. He was recognized as one of the most popular and widely read Soviet writers, appreciated by the general public, as well as Party officials. In his lifetime he had been awarded some of the most prestigious Soviet prizes: the Stalin prize (1950), the Lenin prize (1965), and "The Badge of Honor" (1975).

Despite his popularity Trifonov never attracted sufficient attention from literary critics who responded to some of his individual works but seldom made an attempt to examine general tendencies in his writing. Moreover, the critics tended to focus their attention on sociological questions, such as the correlation between Trifonov's portrayal of life and actual Soviet reality, the problem of petit-bourgeois mentality, or the lack of positive models. Only infrequently did they provide some insight into the artistic qualities of his works, analyzing their generic characteristics, compositional and narrative structure, or stylistic peculiarities. One such rare exception is a study entitled *The Prose of Yury Trifonov*, written by a Soviet scholar Natalia Ivanova and published in Moscow in 1984.[1] Ivanova's book explores the social relevance of Trifonov's prose as well as its artistic coherence.

The only other book devoted entirely to Trifonov was published in the United States by Tatiana Patera.[2] Her *Survey of the Works of Yury Trifonov and an Analysis of His Moscow Novellas* is concerned primarily with the problem of allusion and Aesopian language in the writer's major works, and intentionally avoids the question of their formal structure.

Patera's monograph was published by Ardis, the publishing house which first introduced Trifonov to the American reader. *The Ardis Anthology of Recent Russian Literature* was published in 1975. It included Trifonov's *The Exchange,* which was re-issued in 1978 along with two other novellas in the collection *The Long Goodbye.* In the 1980s Simon and Shuster published two translations of Trifonov's works: *Another Life. The House on the Embankment* (1983) and *The Old Man* (1984).

Critical response to Trifonov's translations has been very positive. In his review of *The Long Goodbye,* John Updike praised the Soviet writer for his Tolstoyan "incomparably elastic open sense of human nature" and his portrayal of the independence of human spirit.[3] In the review of *Another Life. The House on the Embankment,* Richard Lourie called Trifonov a Soviet Chekhov; he underlined the author's use of telling detail and minute description of everyday life which transmits the belief that "our lives are made of small traces, and all the rest no matter how much harm it does us, really doesn't matter."[4]

The works of Trifonov also attracted the attention of North American scholars who offered some general introductions to his writings as well as detailed studies of his major works. There is, however, no comprehensive study on Trifonov which examines all of his creative works and traces his evolution from the rigid patterns of Socialist Realism towards deep psychological explorations of the moral issues facing contemporary Soviet man.

The purpose of this book is to fill this gap and to discuss Trifonov's entire creative career, from his early novel *Students* and the Turkmenian stories, through his best known Moscow novellas, to his very last, *Time and Place, The Overturned House,* and the unfinished novel *Disappearance.* Emphasis is given to textual analysis and the exploration of his works' compositional and temporal structure, narrative technique and stylistic uniqueness.

In order to establish the distinctive nature of Trifonov's prose, his works will be examined in the context of Socialist Realism, the theory which since 1934 has determined the character and development of Soviet literature. Comparisons will be drawn to the writings of other contemporary Soviet authors, notably Daniil Granin, Vladimir Tendryakov, I. Grekova, Vadim Kozhevnikov, and others.

CHAPTER I

A BIOGRAPHICAL SKETCH

Yury Valentinovich Trifonov was born on August 28, 1925, and spent his first twelve years in the comfortable surroundings of a government house in Moscow and a country cottage in Serebryannyi Bor, a cooperative organized by government officials. His father, Valentin Andreevich, was an old-guard Bolshevik who joined the Communist Party in 1904, was exiled four times to Siberia, participated in two Revolutions, and was one of the organizers of the Red Army, working first for the Chief Headquarters in Petrograd, then moving to the Southern and Caucasian Fronts. Following the Civil War, Valentin held many responsible jobs, among them the chairmanship of the Oil Syndicate, the military mission in China, and diplomatic service in Finland, and his family enjoyed all the privileges which came with these high positions.[5]

This way of life ended for Yury on June 22, 1937, when his father was arrested, and the family was forced to move from the exclusive "house on the embankment" into a small apartment near Central Park.[6] His father perished in the purges, and his mother was arrested and exiled for eight years, leaving Yury and his sister with a grandmother. Following the outbreak of the Second World War, the family was evacuated to Tashkent, where Yury attended high school. Upon graduation in 1942, he returned to Moscow and volunteered for the front, but was rejected on account of his poor eyesight. He began working at the Aircraft Factory, first as a fitter, and later as a shop controller.[7]

In 1944, Trifonov entered Gorky Literary Institute, where he studied creative writing, something he had been fascinated with since early childhood. Already at the age of thirteen he had attended a literary club at the Pioneers' House and had written science fiction stories. In his autobiographical "The Prolonged Lessons" (Prodolzhitel'nye uroki), written many years later, he confesses:

> I was incurably sick with writers' itch. Sometimes I would jump out of bed at night, sit at the table and in a somnambulistic state write ten or so pages of science fiction. I was trying to catch up with Levka; after all he'd been writing novels since grade five, and I had just started.[8]

In the same article, Trifonov speaks of the lasting influence made on him by Konstantin Paustovsky, one of his teachers in the Gorky Literary Institute. He recollects Paustovsky's favorite saying, "There is nothing more difficult than a writer's work," which seemed like "a romantic exaggeration" at the time, but over time turned out to be true.

As a student in the Institute, Trifonov made his literary debut in 1947, publishing a short sketch about student life entitled "The Wide Range" (Shirokii diapazon).[9] A year later he published two short stories: "Familiar Places" (Znakomye mesta) and "In the Steppe" (V stepi).[10]

In 1949 Trifonov wrote his first novel *Students* (Studenty), which was accepted as his graduating thesis at the Institute, and serialized in the leading Soviet literary journal, *Novy Mir.*[11] The novel became an instant success, in part because of its interesting subject matter—student life in post-war Moscow—but largely owing to its lively presentation of this material. The novel was well received by critics, and won the prestigious Stalin prize for literature in 1951. Within a decade, it had gone through several printings and had been translated into many foreign languages. In 1952 it was adapted into a play entitled *The Years of Youth* (Molodye gody), which was staged in the Moscow Ermolova Theater.

In 1953 the same theater staged Trifonov's play *A Pledge of Success* (Zalog uspekha), but the play received bad reviews and was soon withdrawn from the program.[12] The reviewers pointed out the discrepancy between the logical development of the plot, which depicts the degradation of a young painter, Andrei Karpukhin, who wastes his talent for easy money and luxuries, and the improbable happy ending, which features his sudden change and return to his early ideals. The critic V. Sappak wrote that the play lacked psychological motivation and made the viewer doubt the change in Karpukhin's character.

The sharp criticism of *A Pledge of Success* must have been very disappointing to Trifonov, who had achieved such success with his first novel. He was unable to write anything new to match his first novel without repeating its pattern. As a remedy, he undertook a trip to Turkmenia, hoping that the new experience and new impressions would give him suitable material. He visited the construction site of the Kara-Kum canal, and upon his return to Moscow began to write a novel about it, but he had to abandon his work when the construction project was declared unprofitable and terminated. The Soviet critic A. Bocharov noted that this experience taught the young writer that "a contemporary theme, usually considered a sure winner, could sometimes be treacherous."[13]

The time spent and the experience gained from that trip were not, however, totally wasted. Trifonov used the material gathered in Turkmenia for many of his short stories, published first in the magazine *Znamya*, then collected in the book *Under the Sun* (Pod solntsem).[14] These stories depict the impressions of a young Moscow journalist who is overwhelmed during his first visit to Turkmenia by the contrasts between the old and the new, between ancient customs and modern methods of conquering the desert. The stories effectively convey the local color, interspersing it with a documentary-like account of the changes taking place in Soviet Turkmenia: the construction of canals, oil explorations, the building of new cities and towns. "There is nothing stronger than man's stubbornness. Sooner or later the deserts of the world will experience it," Trifonov wrote in his introduction to the stories, and these words could be used as a motto for the entire cycle.

In the late 1950s and early 1960s Trifonov frequently traveled abroad, sometimes as a tourist, but more often as a sports correspondent. He attended soccer championships in Hungary and Spain, and the Olympic Games in Rome and Innsbruck; he depicted his impressions in numerous short stories and essays, sketches and notes, published first in the sports magazines *Sovetskii sport* and *Futbol*, and later in book form in *At the End of the Season* (V kontse sezona) and *Bonfires and Rain* (Kostry i dozhd').[15] He also wrote a script for the movie *The Hockey Players* (Khokeisty), produced by Mosfilm in 1964.

In 1963 Trifonov published his second novel, *The Quenching of Thirst* (Utolenie zhazhdy), dedicated to the Kara-Kum canal he had visited ten years earlier.[16] Fortunately for Trifonov, the construction of the canal had been resumed in 1958 and successfully completed a year later, thus enabling the writer to finish the novel and publish it. *The Quenching of Thirst* was written in the tradition of the "industrial" novel: it described the construction of the canal in terms of technical problems and the clashes that arose from different attitudes toward labor, but the industrial theme was complemented by the theme of the moral renewal in Soviet life which resulted from the de-Stalinization policy. The title of the novel refers not only to a thirst for water, but also to a thirst for justice in reevaluating the recent past. *The Quenching of Thirst* was Trifonov's second major success, matching that of *Students;* the novel went through five printings within a decade, and was nominated for the Lenin prize in 1965.[17] A year earlier Trifonov, together with A. Morov, adapted the novel for the stage, and it was successfully staged at the Ashkhabad Russian Theater, Sverdlovsk Drama Theater, and Moscow Gorky Theater. In 1965, Trifonov transformed the novel into a film script, the production of which was directed by B. Mansurov at the Turkmenian Film Studios.

In 1965 *Znamya* published Trifonov's *Reflection of the Fire* (Otblesk kostra), a documentary work about his father and uncle, Valentin and Evgeny Trifonov, who had dedicated their lives to the cause of the Bolshevik revolution.[18] *Reflection of the Fire* depicts their orphan childhood in Maikop, their involvement in the Rostov revolt of 1905, their subsequent exiles and escapes, and their participation in the 1917 Revolution and the Civil War. A great deal of attention is devoted to the years 1918-21, when Valentin served in the Military Tribunal in the South, in the Urals and on the Caucasian Fronts, and Evgeny worked as a commissar on the Southern Front and later in Uzbekistan. The book briefly mentions their careers in the 1920s, during which Valentin was chairman of the Oil Syndicate and did diplomatic work in China and Finland, and Evgeny studied at the Military Academy and directed the Revolutionary Theater. The book fails, however, to elucidate their response to the Stalinist purges of political, military and artistic circles in the 1930s. Both Valentin and Evgeny fell victims to those purges: the former was arrested on the night of June 22, 1937, and disappeared without a trace, while the latter died of a heart attack in December of the same year, apparently while awaiting arrest.

Reflection of the Fire and *The Quenching of Thirst* were both published in the literary magazine *Znamya*, where Trifonov also published his Turkmenian stories "Roads in the Desert." In the mid-sixties Trifonov switched from the conservative *Znamya* to the more radical and prestigious *Novy Mir,* which had earlier serialized his first novel, *Students.* Trifonov returned to *Novy Mir* with a series of short stories that included "Vera and Zoika" (Vera i Zoika), "A Summer Midday" (Byl letnii polden'), "In an Autumn of Mushrooms" (V gribnuiu osen'), and "The Smallest Town" (Samyi malen'kii gorod).[19] The new stories were distinguished by new themes as well as new forms. First of all, the author turned his attention to contemporary urban life, selecting for his stories everyday occurrences that allow the protagonists to reveal their true characters. The plots of these stories remain extremely simple, but their denouements surprise the reader with unexpected twists and possibilities for a variety of interpretations. Despite their laconic style, many of these stories resemble compact novellas, posing important questions of moral values and responsibilities.

Indeed, the stories of the sixties marked a transition to a novelistic genre, which became prominent in Trifonov's writing in the next decade. The first novella of what is usually called Trifonov's Moscow trilogy appeared in 1969, and was entitled *The Exchange* (Obmen). It was followed in 1970 by *Taking Stock* (Predvaritel'nye itogi), and in 1971 by *The Long Goodbye* (Dolgoe proshchanie).[20] All three novellas, as well as *Another Life* (Drugaia zhizn') were published in *Novy Mir*, indicating that the dismissal of Alexander Tvardovsky from the post of editor-in-chief did not change Trifonov's attitude toward the journal.[21] Despite obvious differences in their subjects and structure, the Moscow novellas display a great deal of similarity. First, they all depict the milieu of the urban intelligentsia and place their protagonists against the background of everyday life. The central conflict emerges from the inner struggle between opposing values in the protagonists' minds. Characteristically, that struggle is presented by a concealed narrator who transmits the points of view of the characters themselves, without interference from the omniscient author. The critic A. Bocharov defined Trifonov's technique as "x-raying" life by exploring the psyche of the heroes, rather than merely depicting the details of everyday life.[22]

The publication of the Moscow novellas generated a heated controversy among Trifonov's readers and critics. Some acknowledged his skill in the psychological portrayal of characters and praised him for conveying the dramatic essence of everyday reality.[23] Many, however, criticized him for a preoccupation with mundane details, which, they felt, led to an imbalanced depiction of reality and a lack of positive characters.[24] The latter criticism angered the writer and he answered his critics in the article "To Choose, to Decide, to Sacrifice" (Vybirat', reshat'sia, zhertvovat'), in which he argued against the artificial division of characters into positive or negative. "A human being", maintained Trifonov, "is a combination of subtle threads, and not a piece of wire switched on to a positive or negative current."[25]

"To Choose, to Decide, to Sacrifice" is one of several articles that Trifonov wrote in the late sixties and early seventies which disclose his views on literature and literary craftsmanship. In "The Return to Prosus" (Vozvrashchenie k Prosus) he questions the idea of clear boundaries between a short story and a novella, stressing that both genres are equally capable of grasping life and that what really matters is the inner development that can make a five-page story equivalent to a thick epic.[26] In the same article, he argues against considering plot the most important aspect of prose, though he admits that he was strongly attached to it in his early writing.

In "An Endless Beginning" (Neskonchaemoe nachalo) he distinguishes three phases in his own career: plot-oriented literature, as in *Students;* descriptive literature, searching for the "right word," in the Turkmenian stories; and the "meaningful" literature of the sixties and seventies:

> It seems to me that the main difficulty of prose is to find thoughts. It does not mean that a writer has to strive for profundity and convey aphorisms in every paragraph, but he has to say something, to tell the reader something important.[27]

In all the above articles Trifonov reveals a great deal about himself, his works and his way of writing. He speaks about difficulties in finding the right beginning, the necessity to change details in the process of writing, and the continuous search for the maximum degree of truthfulness in transmitting a depicted reality. He also pays tribute to those who had the greatest impact on his writings: classical geniuses of Russian literature, like Dostoevsky and Chekhov, and those contemporary writers who acted as his teachers and advisers, like Konstantin Paustovsky and Alexander Tvardovsky.[28]

While working on those novellas which deal with contemporary life in the Soviet Union, Trifonov made a venture into the past and wrote a novel entitled *Impatience* (Neterpenie) about the nineteenth-century Russian revolutionary movement called "The People's Will."[29] Commissioned by the "Politizdat" Publishing House for the series "Ardent Revolutionaries," the novel deals primarily with the terrorist Andrei Zhelyabov. The novel begins when Zhelyabov joins the conspiratory group and breaks with his family. It covers the years of his terrorist activities in St. Petersburg, together with his lover, Sofia Perovskaya, and ends with the crushing of "The People's Will" and the execution of its leaders in 1881.

In portraying Zhelyabov and his comrades, Trifonov relies primarily on historical facts, but occasionally introduces fictional material that strengthens the psychological portraits of the protagonist and his colleagues. In addition to the narrator's voice, he uses the voices of secondary characters to introduce facts that would have been inaccessible to the protagonists, as well as the informative sections titled "Clio 72" that evaluate the historical events of the novel from the perspective of contemporary times.

Trifonov's preoccupation with the distant historical past did not last very long. After completing *Impatience* he returned to contemporary themes, publishing his novella *Another Life* in 1975, and *The House on the Embankment* (Dom na naberezhnoi) in 1976.[30] The latter work appeared in *Druzhba narodov*, a rather obscure literary magazine which drastically changed its profile in the 1970s by publishing such controversial works as Vladimir Tendryakov's *The Eclipse*, Fazil Iskander's *Revenge*, and Evgeny Popov's *Stories*.[31] It is hard to determine the exact reasons for Trifonov's switch to *Druzhba narodov*, but one can speculate that, in submitting his works to a more liberal journal, the writer was demonstrating his disapproval of the growing conservatism of *Novy Mir*. Trifonov's cooperation with *Druzhba narodov* lasted until the end: in 1978 he published the novel *The Old Man* (Starik) and in 1981 the journal posthumously published Trifonov's last novel, *Time and Place: A Novel in Thirteen Chapters* (Vremia i mesto: Roman v trinadtsati glavakh).[32]

The appearance of *The House on the Embankment* marked a turning point in Trifonov's career: the writer began to move beyond the novella structure toward a more complex novelistic genre based on a multitude of narrative voices, an extended temporal framework, and a fragmented composition which loosened the causal and chronological ties between individual parts. The first step in this direction was taken by Trifonov in *The House on the Embankment*, which traces the spiritual development of the careerist Vadim Glebov. The novel covers a time span of almost forty years. It dwells extensively on various periods in Glebov's life, beginning with his childhood in the late 1930s, then going on to his studies at the university a decade later, and finally, his successful academic career in the mid-seventies. In addition to the main narrative voice of Glebov himself, the novel transmits the voice of a childhood friend, which allows the reader to form a more objective view of Glebov.

The Old Man has a wider thematic range than *The House on the Embankment* and covers a more impressive span of sixty years. Trifonov's favorite theme of the development of a character during changing times and circumstances appears here also. *The Old Man* reflects on the Bolshevik Revolution and the Civil War and their effects on the formation of Pavel Letunov, the protagonist of the novel. Acting as the central narrator, Letunov goes back to the years of his childhood before the Revolution, but concentrates on the years of the Civil War and his encounter with the Cossack commander Mironov. The historical layer is combined in the novel with contemporary events of the 1970s, and here Letunov's narrative voice is complemented by the voices of two more characters, which bring in new perspectives and throw new light on the events.

The structure of *Time and Place* is even more complex: it compresses vast epic material, covering a span of nearly fifty years, with a multitude of characters and events, into a narrow framework of thirteen chapters, narrated by two narrators who are not clearly distinguished from each other. Moreover, the thirteen chapters are loosely connected, and the events do not unfold gradually, in a consecutive order, but casually and abruptly, without a transition from one chapter to the next, leaving the reader to wonder what has happened in the meantime.

Time and Place appeared in the September and October issues of *Druzhba narodov*, two months after *Novy Mir* had published a series of Trifonov's short stories entitled *The Overturned House* (Oprokinutyi dom).[33] The six stories comprising the series have a common source—the writer's impressions from his frequent visits abroad, including his trips to France, Italy, Finland and the United States. Despite the diversity of the material and plots the stories have common themes: the purpose of life, the passing of time, and the inevitability of death. The mood is reflective and profound. These stories were written shortly before Trifonov's death, and in retrospect their focus on death and the best ways to face it is striking to the reader.

Trifonov died unexpectedly on March 28, 1981, as a result of complications following a rather minor kidney operation. His death at the age of fifty-five cut short a literary career that was marked by constant change and the desire to convey the essence of changing times. In an interview with a correspondent from *Literaturnaya gazeta* Trifonov pointed out:

> There is one factor that justifies all of us who are trying to compete with great writers. It is Time, which we are obliged to transmit in our books according to our ability. Unfortunately, neither Tolstoy nor Chekhov can do it for us. It is our task.[34]

CHAPTER II

STUDENTS

Published in 1950 in *Novy Mir*, Trifonov's first novel *Students* is one of several works devoted to the life of students in post-war Moscow.[35] Others include G. Konovalov's *The University*, V. Dobrovolsky's *The Three in Gray Coats* and *Zhenya Maslova*, and K. Lokotkov's *Fidelity*.[36] In accordance with the requirements of Socialist Realism, these novels depict student life as a collective, governed by common intentions and a common purpose: to learn as much as possible in the Institute in order to become a useful member of society after graduation. Typical conflicts introduced in these novels deal with the struggle between the principles of the collective and individualism as well as the personal problems of the protagonists, whether these be difficulties in their academic work or complications in their personal lives. Characteristically, the conflicts are resolved happily; straying individuals return to the collective and over-come their personal problems.

As a product of its times, *Students* follows the typical model very closely. It develops the theme of student life by portraying the collision of two different attitudes: honest, hard work within the collective and self-ish, egocentric individualism that serves only personal interests. These two attitudes are exemplified in the novel by two characters, Vadim Belov, a modest and industrious student, always ready to help others, and Sergei Palavin, a self-centered egotist, interested only in furthering his personal career. The two characters are portrayed as close friends who depend on each other in school, fight in the Second World War, and upon returning to Moscow, enter the Education Institute. But if Vadim chooses the

Institute because of his desire to become a teacher, Sergei thinks that the less prestigious Institute will help him make an academic career. To achieve this end, Sergei is ready to use any means, including plagiarism and feigned friendship with a professor who can help him.

Sergei's negative qualities are disclosed in the novel gradually, through the eyes of Vadim. Cast as the positive character, Vadim is depicted as an antipode to Sergei: modest rather than self-assured, hard-working rather than brilliant, ready to help others rather than take advantage of the situation. Unlike Sergei, Vadim is shown to be deeply involved in the life of the student collective, participating in such Komsomol-sponsored activities as cooperation with the Literary Club in the Machine Building Factory and volunteer work at the construction of a new residential project. His involvement is devoid of any personal benefits; he works for the sake of principles.

Because he is extremely honest himself, Vadim is slow to recognize the true nature of his best friend, but when he does, he speaks out openly against him at a students' meeting. Such a drastic confrontation is intended to emphasize that real friendship depends on open criticism rather than cover-up and support. The conflict between the two friends is heightened by the motif of their rivalry for the affection of their fellow student Lenochka Medovskaya. She is first courted by Vadim, but eventually leaves him for Sergei, a man far more fascinating than his dull, dutiful friend. The love triangle is a minor conflict, however, designed to throw additional light on the characters rather than to move along the plot.

The second conflict in the novel involves a confrontation between the student body and a professor who is oblivious to the students' needs and preoccupied with his own narrow interests. Portrayed as the villain of the novel, Professor Kozelsky is described as a "formalist" and "cosmopolitan," fascinated by biographical and factual data at the expense of a deeper analysis of the general development of literature. He appears as an admirer of Western and nineteenth-century Russian literatures, totally ignorant of the new developments in contemporary Soviet fiction. As the supervisor of the Student Research Society, he forces the students to write about classical Russian literature and discourages them from approaching Soviet writers. In exams, he pursues trivial facts and fails students who have dared to criticize him in the past. The conflict between Kozelsky and the students, which is introduced at the beginning of the novel, reaches its climax in the middle when, in response to the students' criticism, the dean asks for Kozelsky's resignation. The figure of the dean, meant to provide a positive contrast to Kozelsky, is sketched in such general terms that it fails to come to life.

Similar shortcomings, i.e., generalization and schematism, weaken the

portrayal of most of the minor characters appearing in the novel. These
are simplistically divided into positive and negative types. Most of the students are depicted positively. Among the positive characters number the
dedicated Komsomol chairman, Spartak Galustian, the hard-working
Andrei Syrykh, who came to the Institute straight from the factory, the
hot-tempered but responsive ex-sailor Pyotr Lagodenko, and his wife
Rita.

Lena Medovskaya stands out among the negative characters. She is an
empty-headed beauty, preoccupied with her looks and totally disinterested either in serious work or Komsomol activities. Lena appears in the
novel as Sergei's spiritual sister: self-centered and egotistic, conceited and
vain. Like Sergei, she acquired her superiority complex at home, where
she was spoiled by her mother and became convinced that she was better
and more talented than others. In her concern with her looks and her
preoccupation with finding the right husband, Lena reminds one of the
stereotypical heroine of popular Western romantic novels.[37]

The great number of characters appearing in *Students* underlines an
important aspect of the novel: the portrayal of the student collective. The
novel offers numerous descriptions of events involving large groups of
students, such as the meetings of the Student Society, examinations, and
life in the student dormitory. An event of particular importance is
depicted in chapter 11, in which students participate in a "subbotnik,"
volunteer Saturday labor which involves digging ditches for the gas pipes
in a new residential district. In a manner typical of the literature of the
period, Trifonov emphasizes the young people's enthusiasm for manual
labor and the satisfaction they receive from performing it.

The second important project depicted at length in the novel concerns
the cooperation between the students and the workers who organize a
Literary Club in the Machine Building Factory. The students come to the
Club's meetings, give talks on Soviet literature, and discuss the creative
works of the local members. As with physical labor, the cooperation with
workers is shown to be a source of satisfaction and fulfillment.

Predictably, the volunteer work depends on the involvement of positive characters such as Vadim, Andrei, and Spartak. In contrast, the negative characters, such as Sergei or Lena, shy away from this type of work
unless it is of personal benefit to them. Thus, Sergei goes to the factory to
gather material for his industrial novel, but excuses himself from future
visits by faking illness. Lena uses the same excuse when she refuses to take
part in the "subbotnik."

Portrayed throughout the novel as individualistic and self-centered,
both Sergei and Lena undergo a radical transformation toward the end of
the narrative. After staying at home for a week, Sergei realizes the dread-

fulness of being alone and returns to the Institute. With the help of Vadim he begins the process of reassimilation into the collective. Similarly, Lena, shown until now as an empty-headed beauty, proves herself to be a talented student teacher, easily establishing a rapport with pupils and getting involved in their extra-curricular activities. An even more unexpected "rehabilitation" occurs with Professor Kozelsky, who admits his mistakes and is reinstated at the University.

Such a happy resolution of all the major conflicts was in accordance with the "conflict-free" literature that reigned in the late 1940s. Following the premise that Soviet reality was free from basic social conflicts, writers portrayed "conflict-free" situations and emphasized the general movement from "good" to "better." If they did introduce any conflicts, they made sure that all of them were resolved happily in the end.[38]

In view of the above, it is surprising that many reviewers of *Students* were critical of its happy ending, considering it unwarranted by the logical development of characters. A. Lozhechko wrote in *Oktyabr*:

> One cannot believe this [transformation]. The reader does not see Sergei's inner struggle, his overcoming of those qualities that were rejected by his friends. Sergei's inner change is actually not described. The author restricts himself to depicting Sergei's participation in a volleyball game; this scene symbolizes Sergei's return to the collective, but his return is not motivated artistically, nor is it justified by the logic of the character's development, and therefore it is not convincing.[39]

The critic also disapproved of the sudden transformation of Professor Kozelsky, pointing out that "in order to change his outlook and inner character, this man would have to suffer a lot. And this is not shown in the novel."[40] B. Galanov expressed a similar opinion; he accused Trifonov of making a serious mistake in approaching Professor Kozelsky with an optimistic hypothesis:

> The transformation of this pseudo-scientist is too quick. His telephone conversation with Palavin about his reappraisal of values is an unmotivated attempt on the part of the author to rehabilitate Kozelsky and thereby resolve one more conflict[41]

Both critics reproached the author for the weak individualization of some of the characters, especially the positive ones. In their view, both the dean, intended as a positive counterpart to Kozelsky, and Olga, who replaces Lena in Vadim's affection, remain sketches rather than fully developed characters. The characterization of Vadim, the positive hero of the novel, also struck the critics as unconvincing. "Unfortunately," Lozhechko wrote, "his image is not finished; Vadim is honest and hard-working, but his goals are not revealed, and therefore seem narrow. His dreams seem pale and barren, and his mind—dull."[42]

The reviewers were not all like-minded in their criticism of the novel. Some praised Trifonov for his convincing depiction of the student milieu,[43] while others criticized him for not revealing the inner life of the students, the formation of their characters in relation to their academic experience.[45] B. Galanov complained about the superficial depiction of the faculty members, who, after all, should be mentors rather than antag-onists. Whereas the majority of commentators spoke favorably of the freshness and originality in Trifonov's depiction of student life, some rep-rimanded him for using too many colloquialisms and slang expressions.[45]

While pointing out the shortcomings of *Students*, the critics, neverthe-less, encouraged the young writer to continue to work on the novel and revise it. But Trifonov refused to do so, preferring to seek new ideas and to transform them into different literary forms. Thirty years later, he spoke of the change he underwent after finishing his first novel:

> Along with changes in life and in living conditions, my attitude had changed as well. And I also had become more experienced and mature. I wanted to find a new key to understanding reality and a new style. That is why I tried to move away from *Students*.[46]

CHAPTER III

SHORT STORIES OF THE 1950S:

UNDER THE SUN

&

AT THE END OF THE SEASON

Following the publication of *Students*, Trifonov found himself in the difficult position of not being able to write anything new. His period of silence lasted several years and was finally broken in 1956 with the appearance of three stories: "Doctor, Student and Mitya" (Doktor, student i Mitia), "The Last Hunt" (Posledniaia okhota), and "At the End of the Season" (V kontse sezona).[47] These three stories marked a new period in Trifonov's work that was to last for almost a decade. First of all, the writer abandoned the novelistic genre, at least for the time being, and turned to the short story. Secondly, he renounced plot as the most important aspect of a literary work and concentrated on style. "Each word is like a heavy truck," Trifonov emphasized in his article "An Endless Beginning" (Neskonchaemoe nachalo), "burdened with a huge load of meaning, sometimes double or triple. There are no empty trucks."[48] Thirdly, he introduced two new themes into his writings: Soviet Central Asia and the changes taking place there, and achievements in sport. These themes reflect, respectively, the new experience he had gained from his trip to Turkmenia and his life-long passion for sports.

"Doctor, Student and Mitya" and "The Last Hunt," Trifonov's first stories about Turkmenia, were followed by an entire series, first published in 1959 in *Znamya* as "Roads in the Desert" and later in book form as *Under the Sun* (Pod solntsem).[49] The book contained several more stories than the journal, arranged in a different sequence, but with the same framework, depicting the arrival of a young Moscow journalist to Turkmenia and his subsequent departure. Since a Moscow journalist comes from a different background and a different culture, he should be able to see Turkmenia in a fresh and original way, unspoiled by established norms or habits. The reader might expect a great deal of "estrangement," which, according to Viktor Shklovsky, makes objects unfamiliar and strange by distorting them and showing them from a different perspective.[50] Indeed, the device of "estrangement" does appear in Trifonov's stories, but on the whole it is subordinated to the documentary-like tendency to depict things the way they were, or rather the way they were supposed to be depicted in Soviet literature. Thus the stories emphasize the changing landscape of the country, which reflects the process of industrialization and modernization: the oil towers, the new towns, the construction of an irrigation canal. More importantly, the stories convey the idea of sweeping change in people's lifestyles: from unskilled peasants to skillful miners and power-shovel operators ("Under the Sun" and "Five Years Ago"), from enslaved girls to emancipated women working in the collective and participating in local music festivals ("Festival in Mary"), from nomadic herdsmen to retired members of a collective who receive state pensions ("The Sand Clock").

The most notable feature of the Turkmenian stories is the absence of a well-developed plot connecting a series of episodes temporally and causally. Instead, the stories describe a single episode or a single character, as seen or observed by the narrator. In all but two stories the narrator acts as the main storyteller who reports what he has witnessed and presents his interpretation of events. As might be expected, the narrator appears as a biased witness, evaluating everything from his point of view and imposing his perspective on the reader. But at the same time, he presents an immediate and direct account of events, thus convincing the reader of their authenticity and truthfulness.

In conveying his impressions of Turkmenia, the narrator concentrates primarily on the depiction of people he had met during his travels and who had struck him as extraordinary. Thus, he portrays Shaturdy, a young Turkmenian herdsman who within five years became an assistant supervisor of the oil drilling ("Five Years Ago"), the young biologist Galya, who learned how to cope with the difficult life in the desert ("The Eyeglasses"); and two herpetologists fascinated with their work in the Kara-Kum desert ("A Chat with Herpetologists"). According to the standards of Soviet literature, all the above protagonists are positive characters, dedicated to their work and not concerned about personal inconveniences and adversities. Alongside them, Trifonov depicts negative characters who do not appreciate the idealistic goals of the collective and work for their own gains. Such is the excavator machinist Evseev ("Under the Sun"), the barber Bako ("Bako"), and the wrestler Klych Durda, who earns his living from "play" rather than from serious work ("The Loneliness of Klych Durda").

As a rule, Trifonov reveals his characters in one episode and one situation. Klych Durda's loneliness is shown in a scene that depicts his fight for the local championship, where the entire audience is against him, considering him an idler. Significantly, Trifonov portrays his protagonist indirectly, through the audience's comments and attitudes; the narrator simply registers the facts. In a similar way, the narrator in "Under the Sun" presents Evseev's negative qualities, first through the perception of his co-workers and then in a single episode which merely confirms his stinginess.

Occasionally, the narrator introduces the characters with the help of dialogues which allow them to speak directly to the reader. This method of characterization is used in "A Chat with Herpetologists," which consists almost entirely of dialogues between two herpetologists and the narrator, and in "Five Years Ago," in which the narrator transmits the words of the protagonist, who childishly boasts about his achievements in the past five years.

On the whole, the situations and characters portrayed in the Turkmenian stories are static. They give the impression of being captured by a camera, which reveals the typical features of a contemporary man in a still picture, as L. Lazarev cogently observed in his review of *Under the Sun*.[51] Extending Lazarev's metaphor, one could say that only two stories remind the reader of three-dimensional shots made with a movie camera and showing the characters in motion. These are "The Eyeglasses" and "The Poppies." Each depicts a sequence of several episodes and portrays the development of characters. In comparison with the plotless sketches discussed earlier these stories have simple but discernible plots with a clear beginning, climax and denouement. "The Poppies" is a story of a short-lived love, which begins with the arrival of topographs in a distant metereological station, reaches its climax in an encounter between Grisha and Olga, and ends with Grisha's return three months later, when he realizes that his feelings for Olga have vanished. The plot encompasses the events of a day in April when millions of poppies cover the desert, and ends in the middle of July, when the desert is bare and the sand hills resemble empty coffins. The change in the landscape corresponds to the protagonist's change in mood from passionate fascination to indifference.

The temporal frame of "The Eyeglasses" is also very limited. The story covers the events of several days: it begins with the decision to fire Ashir, an assistant to the biologist Galya, continues into the next day, when Galya loses her eyeglasses, and reaches its climax one evening, when she decides to look for them and gets lost in the desert. The denouement comes two days later, when Galya is found and brought back to the camp, where she learns that Ashir will not be fired after all. Unlike "The Poppies," "The Eyeglasses" offers a lengthy exposition, which summarizes Galya's three-month stay in the desert and describes her bewilderment at the people working there: "They are somewhat strange, a motley group. Are they good or bad?" wonders Galya at the beginning of the story. The denouement offers a clear answer to that question: the people in the camp prove to be caring and concerned about one another, even if at risk to their own lives.

Both stories portray the protagonists against the background of several other characters who, despite the brief glimpses given of them, make a lasting impression on the reader. In "The Eyeglasses" we meet the interesting Marya Andreevna, a clear contrast to the inexperienced and naive Galya, as well as other members of the expedition: the man in charge, Malaev; the geodesist, Makhov; and the Turkmenian assistant, Ashir. In "The Poppies" Olga is portrayed among other workers of the meteorological station, such as the strong-willed boss Glafira Stepanovna, her quiet husband, Nikolai Makarovich, and the lonely Faina.

Unlike the other stories in the Turkmenian series "The Poppies" and "The Eyeglasses" are not told by the journalist-narrator, but by a concealed narrator who transmits the protagonist's point of view in his third-person narration. Thus, the story "The Poppies" reflects the point of view of Grisha, who participates in his first field trip to Turkmenia and sees everything as new and exciting. "The Eyeglasses" reproduces the perspective of Galya, a young biologist from Moscow still learning how to cope with the difficult life in the desert and how to understand the people working in those harsh conditions. Significantly, both characters are not only young but also new to the desert, and their perception of life there is not spoiled by routine or habit. Their new experiences, depicted in the stories, not only enrich them, but also change their attitudes towards life and people in general.

In addition to illustrating the multiple facets of a new Turkmenia, Trifonov's stories portray the old lifestyle of the region, vividly demonstrating the progress made in the past thirty years. Thus, in the story "About Water" he depicts Kazakh herdsmen with a caravan of thirty camels searching for pastures, a clear contrast to the cotton-producing collectives described in "The Festival in Mary." In "The Children of Doctor Grisha" he juxtaposes the image of an old Turkmenian quack doctor with that of a bona fide medical doctor, and, interestingly, makes the former show his appreciation for modern medicine by faking a broken leg and forcing the doctor to stay in the area. Many of Trifonov's stories offer glimpses of Turkmenian customs, such as wrestling and the "toi" celebration ("The Loneliness of Klych Durda"), folk singing and dancing ("The Old Song," "The Festival in Mary"), and adherence to the Islamic tradition of fasting and wearing veils ("The Old Men in Kaushuta"). The latter story, which at first strikes the reader as a colorful picture of old Turkmenia, with women dressed in colorful garments and veils and old men sitting idly in front of a tea house, turns out to illustrate again the rapid changes place there. The three old men, who at first seem to personify traditional Islamic values, are truly dedicated to the new system. Two of them had recently captured a criminal who was trying to cross the Iranian border, while the third had killed his brother, who was fighting against the new system.

On the whole, Trifonov is restrained in his inclusion of local color; he avoids long descriptions of folk traditions and the ancient landscape, replacing them with brief, telling details, as in the following passage:

> . . . On the overheated bench three soldiers in dusty, green panamas with holes are wearily waiting for a train. Nearby several female figures move about like a flock of frightened birds...
>
> When we appear, the women stop their twittering and in a single movement cover their mouths with kerchiefs. This is "yashmak," an old tradition: a Turkmenian woman is not supposed to talk to strange men.
>
> But one of the women doesn't move.
>
> "Why, don't you cover yourself with a yashmak," asks Achilov.
>
> The old woman waves her shiny, withered hand: "No one wants my mouth anymore."[52]

Significantly, the old woman speaks in correct, rather than pidgin, Russian, and so do Trifonov's other characters. They either use their own dialect, which the narrator's companion translates for him, or they speak standard Russian, like Shaturdy in "Five Years Ago" or the people from the audience in "The Loneliness of Klych Durda." Very seldom does Trifonov attempt to imitate the broken Russian used by the Turkmenians; a few examples can be found in "The Eyeglasses" in the speech of Ashir's friend or in that of an old land-reclamation engineer in "Doctor, Student, and Mitya."

On the whole, the language of the Turkmenian stories is laconic and resembles the compressed language of newspapers. The narrator who is a journalist, prefers an exact, documentary style to the highly metaphoric language characteristic of many works about Soviet Central Asia. But occasionally the narrator abandons his dry, documentary style and introduces lyrical descriptions of the desert and the people working there.

Thus, he compares walking in the desert to walking in water: "when you walk down the sand hills, your feet sink into the sand up to your ankles. It's like walking in water. The white sand rustles and flows, slipping down in layers" (p. 128). In April, the desert looks like a coral sea: "The evening sun made the sand the orange color of egg-yolk. The sand hills around the station were covered with red foam, with millions of blooming poppies. The bright-red coral sea, burning under the sun's rays, clouded the eyes like blood" (p. 27). In July, the same landscape looks quite different: "The sand was bleached white, and the sand hills around the station were desert-like and bare, like coffins. In a few places you could see dusty bushes" (p. 32).

The people who live and work under the hot sun of the desert are also unique, as may be seen from the description of the three old men in Kaushuta:

> One is thin, with a dark negro-like face and with sharp, piercing eyes. The second is fat and slovenly; he has large, pink ears, slit eyes, and the big lips of a debaucher. The third old man looks like a Persian: his long face is brown, like a chestnut. He has a hooked nose and a gray, goat-like beard. His white eyes blink constantly, and he lifts his head while listening. (p. 118)

Critics received the Turkmenian stories favorably. L. Lazarev praised Trifonov for avoiding unnecessary exotic color and depicting instead the realistic details of life in the desert.[53] He also commended the author for shunning hasty judgments and letting the reader draw his own conclusions. A. Finitskaya gave a similarly positive evaluation of the Turkmenian stories; she spoke of "the new synthesis of psychological insight with an objective documentary, which leads to a fuller presentation of a human character."[54]

Finitskaya's characterization of the Turkmenian cycle can be applied to Trifonov's next book of short stories, published in 1961 by the Sport Publishing House "Physical Education and Sport" and entitled *At the End of the Season* (V kontse sezona).[55] United by the general theme of sport, the stories share another feature: they pose the broader question of the moral issues which the protagonists must face, regardless of their age or their level of achievement. The book portrays a wide range of sports, starting with Trifonov's favorites, soccer and hockey, and ending with the more exotic—wrestling and hunting. But whatever the discipline, the emphasis is on the general attitude and moral standards of sportsmen, rather than on their impressive achievements.

The majority of stories have simple, casual plots, involving one or more episodes, unfolding over a short period of time. The time span of "The Translucent Autumn Sun" (Prozrachnoe solntse oseni) is less than half-an-hour. The two protagonists accidently meet at a Siberian airport, recollect their years at the university twenty years earlier, and part, going in different directions, each convinced that the other has not succeeded in life.[56] The total duration of "At the End of the Season" (V kontse sezona) is thirty-six hours, but the events of one day constitute most of the story, which portrays the attempts of a soccer coach to recruit a talented full-back from a minor league.[57]

Both stories are built around the device of contrast between different personalities and different attitudes. In "The Translucent Autumn Sun" the contrast is in the foreground: both physical and psychological divergences between the protagonists are stressed. Whereas Velichkin is huge and stout, Galetsky is lean and wrinkled; the former is dressed impeccably in a suit and a stylish tie, while the latter wears old, faded ski pants and a jacket that is too short. As befits a worker at a large sport club, Velichkin is self-assured and complacent, while Galetsky, a physical education teacher in a small Siberian town, is shy and self-conscious. In their twenty-minute conversation, they reminisce about their university years and recollect their friends, but, above all, boast about their lives. Velichkin, who frequently travels abroad, brags about clothes and cheap prices, while Galetsky extols his soccer team and one of the players who has been transferred to Moscow. As it turns out, each is fully satisfied with his lot, and feels sorry for the other's "unsuccessful" life. Ironically, in the eyes of the young players, they both appear as "failures," for neither the administrative job nor teaching seems glamorous or rewarding.

The contrast between the two generations and their different expectations is the key element in the story "At the End of the Season," which juxtaposes the idealistic soccer coach Malakhov with the egotistic fullback Buritsky. Malakhov, himself a star in the past, had never succumbed to the temptation to transfer to a bigger city and a better team, but Buritsky accepts the offer without hesitation, disregarding the dreadful consequences for his team. The contrast between the two characters in the story is subdued, and revealed in a single episode, in which Malakhov meets with Buritsky. Too embarrassed to make a straightforward offer, Malakhov reminisces about his past and contemplates his reasons for remaining with the same team. Buritsky, on the other hand, responds in a business-like manner, inquiring about general conditions and the possibility of getting an apartment. The story ends with an unexpected twist: after a sleepless night Malakhov decides not to recruit the promising player and sends his club a brief cable: "Unfortunately no success; fellow's style unacceptable." The word "style" is intentionally ambiguous; to an unsuspicious club chairman it will suggest an unacceptable way of playing soccer, while for Malakhov it describes the player's unacceptable personality.

A different type of contrast underlies the story "The Conqueror of the Swedes" (Pobeditel' shvedov), in which the powerful hockey star Duganov appears as ordinary and defenseless in real life; he not only has problems with his girlfriend Maika, but is on the verge of losing her.[58] Duganov's story is told by a twelve-year-old boy, Alyosha, who is bewildered that his idol is dating the "ordinary" girl living next door. Because Alyosha is the narrator, the hockey in the story is depicted vividly and at length, while relations between Duganov and Maika are restricted to a few details. In the climactic scene of the story, Duganov asks Alyosha to tell Maika to see him after the game. When Maika refuses, Alyosha cannot force himself to tell Duganov the truth. The story has a happy ending, however: Maika finally appears, and Alyosha is relieved and happy.

Of all the stories included in *At the End of the Season*, "The Conqueror of the Swedes" contains the most exciting descriptions of sporting events. Alyosha's fascination with hockey is conveyed in graphic accounts of the game, such as the following:

> ... play erupted like a rocket.
> Sticks banged, the ice squealed, the boards cracked with a dull sound from the strikes. (p. 54)
> There was a continuous cracking, as if several axes were cutting wood, but it was brilliant, fast work, too hard for the eyes to follow. (p. 55)

Occasionally, the style is solemn, reflecting the author's own admiration for hockey:

> Oh, the evening of the Great Game!
> Oh, the glow of projectors above the black rock of the stadium!
> Oh, the holiday, feverish, nervous, unappeasable impatience! Oh, the music from the speakers, cracking and fragile in the frost!
> Oh, contact with the great life of men! (p.53)

Such emotional outbursts about a sport are rare in *At the End of the Season*. On the whole the book is characterized by a simple, laconic style similar to that of *Under the Sun*. Unlike the first collection, the second volume offers few descriptions of nature, unless they are important for the plot. Thus the story "The Stimulus" (Stimul) skillfully depicts the smells and sounds of a forest at night as experienced by a young man hurrying to catch a train.[59] The story successfully evokes the protagonist's growing alarm: his subconscious fear of the forest is sharpened by his encounter with a stranger who pursues him. "The Stimulus", which is told by the protagonist eighteen years later as an illustration of his belief that there is no limit to human potential, reads like a detective story, presenting a spooky experience with a shadowy character in a strained, tense narrative. Like many stories in the collection, it has an unexpected ending: the pursuer turns out to be the protagonist's friend, who is trying to catch up to him to tell him that the train will be arriving the next day.

Elements of a detective story are also present in the story "Far Away in the Mountains" (Daleko v gorakh), in which a young boxer, Alyosha Sychin, is confronted by two bandits attempting to cross the Iranian border.[60] In a climactic scene, Alyosha knocks out one of the bandits, proving to himself, and presumably to the reader, that boxing is important not only in the ring, but also in real life. This naive moral turns this rather interesting work into a simplistic tale, extolling the virtues of determination and strong will.

Set against the background of Soviet Central Asia, the story paints a compelling picture of a devastatingly hot summer which makes Alyosha's efforts even more painful:

> The days were extremely hot. Even in the morning the air was burning: a dry scorching heat was coming from the mountains. (p. 89)
> The stuffy smell of the scorching tar hovered above the road. The sun was hiding behind the mountains, but the heat did not subside. (p. 90)

The collection *At the End of the Season* also includes two stories published earlier in the Turkmenian series: "The Loneliness of Klych Durda" and "The Last Hunt." Thematically both stories belong in this volume: the former depicts the traditional Asiatic art of wrestling, and the latter portrays deer hunting. But stylistically both stories clash with the restrained simplicity of the other stories in the series insofar as they contain elaborate, colorful images of the desert and old Turkmenian customs.

The writer himself, however, chose to include these works in his later collections of sport stories, *Torches above Flaminio* (Fakely nad Flaminio) and *Games at Dusk* (Igry v sumerkakh). Both volumes testify to the writer's continuous interest in sports, which inspired him to write short stories, essays and sketches about them throughout his literary career.[61]

CHAPTER IV

THE QUENCHING OF THIRST

&

THE INDUSTRIAL NOVEL

The Turkmenian theme, first introduced in the short stories of the 1950s, found its full realization in Trifonov's second novel, *The Quenching of Thirst* (Utolenie zhazhdy), which was begun in 1952, but not finished until ten years later.[62] It was initially serialized in 1963 in *Znamya* and published in book form by the prestigious publishing house "Khudozhestvennaia literatura" a year later.

With its theme of the construction of an irrigation canal in Turkmenia, *The Quenching of Thirst* belongs to the popular genre of the industrial novel, which was developed in Soviet literature of the early thirties and flourishes to this day. In the fifty years of its existence, the genre has gone through several transformations, corresponding to changes in the political and cultural climate.

Introduced into literature as a direct response to the First Five-Year Plan, the industrial novel glorified the achievements of heavy industry and the construction of gigantic industrial projects. Thus, Marietta Shaginyan's *The Hydroelectric Station* and Fyodor Gladkov's *Energy* depicted the construction of hydroelectric stations, while Valentin Kataev's *Time, Forward!* and Ilya Erenburg's *The Second Day* glorified the work of a chemical combine and a metallurgical plant, respectively.[63] Regardless of their subjects, however, all these novels provide detailed descriptions of the technology typical for the given industry, and portray the dedicated work of the collective rather than that of individuals. They contain three major types of conflicts, each of which moves the plot in the desired direction: a struggle against nature, which stubbornly resists men's efforts; a struggle against political enemies, who are ready to use any means to stop construction or disrupt a plant's work; and a struggle against the capitalist attitude to labor based on monetary gains, which was to be replaced by conscientious labor for the benefit of all.[64] Characteristically, all these conflicts are resolved happily, making this literature a useful propaganda tool in "raising the mass consciousness and organizing the mass will and enthusiasm for socialist construction."[65]

In the second stage of the industrial novel's development, in the late 1940s and early 1950s, writers continued to use the same model, but with considerable changes. First of all, they eliminated the antagonistic conflict, the struggle with political enemies, as being untypical for Soviet society so many years after the Revolution. Following the same premise, they weakened the second conflict, that of a selfish attitude toward labor, as uncharacteristic of the Soviet people. As a result, the industrial novel, like Soviet literature in general, became "conflict-free," and simply tended to show dedicated workers breaking records and producing more for the country. That tendency was evident in V. Azhaev's *Far Away from Moscow*, V. Kochetov's *The Zhurbins*, B. Gorbatov's *The Donbass*, and many others.[66] In all these works the preoccupation with technology took precedence over the individualization and psychological motivation of characters. Devoid of individual social or psychological background, the characters appeared as lifeless puppets and tended to be all-positive or all-negative. As could be expected, the industrial novels of the 1950s had happy endings: the positive characters overfulfilled the plan and broke records, the negative characters changed their attitude toward labor.

Following the policy of de-Stalinization and the relaxation of cultural life in the mid-fifties, the industrial novel underwent further transformations. The most outstanding change involved the shift from purely technological problems to moral problems connected with labor, such as duty, a conscientious attitude, and high principles. In the insightful words of the Soviet critic L. Terekopian, "technological progress became tied up with moral progress, since only such a unity secures the advancement of society."[67] Along with the change of emphasis came the widening of the industrial theme to include the private and family lives of the protagonists. It became clear that in order to be convincing, a literary character's psychological makeup and family relations had to be shown and not only his professional and social responsibilities. Psychological motivation became an indispensable part of the industrial novel, as important as social determination had been a decade earlier. These new tendencies of the industrial novel were perfectly embodied in such works as Georgy Vladimov's *The Great Ore*, Vadim Kozhevnikov's *Get Acquainted, Baluev*, V. Lipatov's *The Story of Director Pronchatov*, and many others.[68]

It is within this tradition that Trifonov wrote *The Quenching of Thirst*, combining the theme of industrialization with the theme of moral renewal following the death of Stalin. These two themes are closely interwoven in the novel, simultaneously posing two questions: how to build and how to live.

The Quenching of Thirst depicts the construction of the Kara-Kum canal, a project that would change the Turkmenian desert into an agricultural land. As in the early industrial novel, *The Quenching of Thirst* concentrates on the work of the collective, rather than of individuals, which labors with great dedication to expedite the completion of the canal. As rightly pointed out by A. Bocharov, the novel has no single protagonist;[69] instead it depicts the work of the collective, laboring in the extremely harsh conditions of the desert where "after five minutes in the sun, a lizard would cook alive." (p. 15)

The heat is so unbearable that the power shovels can work only in the early morning or in the evening. During the day, the cabins heat up like boilers and one cannot touch the levers with a bare hand. Even more hazardous are sand storms, when the wind fills the air with tons of fine, hot grains, blocking vision and making breathing impossible. To top it off, there are also rattlers and poisonous spiders, ready to attack the men who invade their territory. Despite nature's strong resistance, work on the canal continues: people keep moving sand hills, and build sluices and bridges for the future railroad.

The fight against nature is one of the major conflicts developed in the novel. There is also an industrial conflict which involves the question of how to build the canal: by following the old method of using power shovels and proceeding from one side, or by adopting a new approach of using bulldozers and digging simultaneously from both sides. Each method has its advocates, and depending on their position, they appear as old-fashioned bureaucrats, concerned about their careers and not willing to take any risks, or as daring innovators, ready to take risks in order to finish the canal quickly. The first group includes the project designer, Baskakov; the deputy head of the Ministry of Water Resources, Niyazdudyev; and the chief engineer at the project, Khorev. The second group is represented by the construction director Ermasov, the engineers Karabash and Gokhberg, and the workers Martin Egers, Biashim Muradov and Beki Essenov. Needless to say, it is this group that exemplifies the "right" attitude, for only daring initiative and new methods can secure the fast completion of the canal.

Of all the positive characters in the novel, Ermasov most closely resembles the heroes of the early industrial novel. He belongs to the generation of old guards who without hesitation put their lives into the service of the country even though it required renunciation of personal happiness. In the late 1930s Ermasov served in the army in Turkmenia, fighting against the local counter-revolutionaries. In 1937 he was unjustly arrested and spent several years in a labor camp. Following his release, he remained in Turkmenia, working at different construction projects, among them the construction of the main Turkmenian canal. Realizing that it was an error to build the canal through an uninhabited area, he wrote to the Central Committee and soon the construction was halted. As a director of the Kara-Kum canal Ermasov introduces daring innovations; he moves the machinery deep into the desert and begins digging the canal from both sides, suggesting the idea of creating artificial lakes and dams along the canal's route.

Ermasov's ideas are constantly opposed by the authorities from the Ministry and the chief engineer, Khorev. Introduced as a principal antagonist, Khorev opposes all of Ermasov's ideas, denounces him to the authorities, and writes a condemnatory article for the Ashkhabad newspaper. His role of adversary is somewhat softened, however, by his admission of a secret admiration for Ermasov. Khorev considers Ermasov:

> a person of natural gifts, an outstanding engineering expert, one of the best in the republic, or even in all of Central Asia.... he respects [him] greatly. He admires... his courage, his robustness, and his peasant stubbornness. He loves him like a brother, in spite of all his whims and his insufferable streak of petty tyranny. (p. 103)

The conflict between the old and the new, and the spirit of selflessness and idealism are reinforced in the novel by the images of two workers, Semyon Nagaev and Martin Egers. Both work very hard as power-shovel operators, but whereas Egers is truly dedicated to the project and tries to expedite its completion, Nagaev is interested in earning money. Of the two characters, Nagaev is more fully developed in the novel. He appears at first as a typical shock-worker who overfulfills his quotas and is sought for interviews and awards. Only gradually does the reader learn that his hard work is motivated by personal greed; he simply wants to earn more money and retire. It is his greediness that drives him to work at night and in the worst heat, refusing to relax or rest.

Interested only in his own welfare, Nagaev turns away his helper, the young Turkmenian boy, Byashim Muradov. But Egers takes Byashim onto his team. Under his guidance, Byashim becomes a skillful power-shovel operator. In the novel he reflects the educational value of labor, which turns him from an inexperienced shepherd into a skilled construction worker. Byashim, however, pays a high price for his conversion: he is killed by his in-laws, who are angered by his refusal to pay the traditional "kalym" for his bride.

Byashim's murder evokes the antagonistic conflict of the early industrial novel which inevitably portrayed the opposition of the old, conservative forces to the new ways of life brought by the Revolution. In addition to Byashim's tragic death, *The Quenching of Thirst* depicts the self-sacrificing death of Denis Kuznetsov, who perishes while attempting to cover a breach in the dam. That heroic act of an ex-expatriate, who had returned to the Soviet Union in 1957 and for a long time could not readjust to a new life, provides another example of the positive influence of labor. Surrounded by trust and confidence, Kuznetsov is able to overcome his alienation and become a full-fledged member of the collective. His death symbolizes his total dedication to the project and his readiness to sacrifice his life for the benefit of others.

The two deaths portrayed in the novel introduce some tragic overtones into the narrative, but they do not change the optimistic ending. As befits an industrial novel, *The Quenching of Thirst* ends with the successful completion of the first line of the canal. The epilogue informs the readers about the construction of the second line by a new crew and under new management. Ermasov has left for the Tien Shan mountains to build a gigantic reservoir and has taken many engineers and workers with him. The completion of the canal is entrusted to Karabash, who has proven himself a skillful engineer and a responsible manager.

The Theme of Moral Renewal

Together with the industrial theme, *The Quenching of Thirst* develops the theme of moral renewal which was taking place in the Soviet Union after the death of Stalin.[70] After many years of mistrust and fear, people were finally learning how to trust each other, and how to "quench" their thirst for justice. In addition to its literal meaning, the title of the novel refers to "the quenching of the thirst for justice," and raises the crucial question of how to achieve it: in a sweeping action or gradually, step by step. In one of the climactic scenes, the following discussion takes place:

> "There is a thirst stronger than the thirst for water, it's the thirst for justice! The restoration of justice!"
> "The party is working on it."
> "The party is working on it, and you? And what about you?" Tamara shouted, and her eyes became small and angry. "Why don't you want to help the party? Do you think that the effects of the cult

of personality..."

"Why are you shouting?" asked the director of city planning. "Do you know how the Turkmenians quench thirst? Just listen: at first, they quench 'a small thirst,' by drinking two or three cups, and after supper, when the kettle is ready, they quench 'a large thirst.' And they never give too much water to a man who's come from the desert. They give a little at a time."

"Otherwise it will harm him," Platon Kiryanovich said.

"Oh, no. No one will be hurt! It's nonsense! I don't believe it," Tamara replied excitedly. "How could there be *too much* truth? Or *too much* justice?" (p. 233).

The people participating in the above discussion are journalists working for the Ashkhabad newspaper *Kopetdagskaya zarya*. Their conflict reflects the opposition of the older, dogmatic thinking, typical of Stalinist times, to a new attitude based on openness and trust. The positions taken are related to the job and the age of the people on the editorial board. The editor-in-chief, Diomidov, and the managing editor, Luzgin, are products of the old times, faithfully following orders from above and afraid to make independent decisions. But whereas Diomidov is a victim of the Stalinist period, governed by fear and indecisiveness, Luzgin actively superimposes his judgment on others and refuses to accept other points of view. For years Luzgin has run the newspaper with a firm hand, without consultations or discussions, expecting everyone to follow him blindly. He is unwilling to change, and in the end has to resign to make room for a more open-minded editor.

The new attitude towards journalism, based on more objectivity and honesty, is represented in the novel by the younger generation, which includes the editor of the literary section, Victor Kritsky; the industrial reporter, Zhorik Tumanian; and the youngest member of the board, Pyotr Koryshev. Koryshev, who has just joined the newspaper, most clearly exemplifies the new trends in Soviet life following the death of Stalin. First of all, he is no longer considered unreliable as "the son of an enemy of the people," since his father was posthumously rehabilitated in 1955. After several years of working in an obscure provincial newspaper, he is given a responsible job as a reporter and eventually becomes editor of the literary section. As a reporter, Koryshev is inquisitive and impartial, striving toward objectivity and refusing blindly to follow the direction of his superiors. As an editor, he proves to be a fair critic, accepting works of true literary value for publication and refusing to support mediocrity and shallowness.

Despite all these positive characteristics, Koryshev, however, is not a perfect "positive" hero. He lacks a strong will and the motivation to achieve his potential as a writer and to arrange his personal affairs in a satisfactory manner. In his own estimation, he is too weak to find his own path and simply follows the general "current":

> My weakness is that I give in, not to someone else, and not even to myself, but to a current which carries me like a chip, tosses and turns me, casts me onto the shore, and then washes me away again and takes me along. And I simply drift. (p. 208).

Basically honest, although weak, Koryshev is contrasted in the novel with the cynical and ruthless Sasha Zurabov, his friend from the university. Sasha, who was then expected to become a successful journalist or writer, had turned into a mediocre reporter, working according to established rules and avoiding any controversial issues. Determined to preserve the existing status quo, he refuses to take a definite stand on the crucial questions of the newspaper's policies and the manner in which it is run.

Despite the resistance of Sasha and his like-minded colleagues, the newspaper does change its profile, opening its pages to controversial issues and "forbidden" authors. The conflict between the old and the new is resolved in favor of the latter; the dictatorial managing editor is replaced by an open-minded liberal; Pyotr Koryshev is promoted to the head of the literary section, and the newspaper in general becomes more open and objective.

Style and Narrative Method

The themes of the construction of the canal and work on the newspaper are developed in the novel along two narrative lines. These two lines function independently; the action moves back and forth from the construction site to the newspaper office, from the Kara-Kum desert to Ashkhabad. Occasionally, however, the two lines intersect. Several times the journalists visit the construction site and report the progress on the work to their readers. Among those who are sent to report on the construction are Zurabov and Koryshev, each coming to the canal at the crucial moment of the completion of the first line. But whereas Zurabov writes a negative report, outlining the mismanagement of machinery, Koryshev stresses the positive side of the construction: the enthusiasm and dedication of the workers, the daring initiatives of the management.

In addition to the journalistic accounts of the construction, the newspaper publishes reports submitted by people directly involved in the project. These include a report by the engineer Khorev, which points out the shortcomings of the project, as well as an open letter by the director Ermasov, defending the use of unorthodox methods. Thus, the topic of the construction figures prominently in the pages of the newspaper, and the paper takes great interest in reporting the progress of the canal.

The two plot lines are also interconnected in the novel through the personal relations of some of the protagonists. Zurabov's wife Lera works at the canal as a biologist and offers a personal account of the construction to her husband and his fellow journalists. Her husband, in turn, reacts negatively to the project when he learns about Lera's unfaithfulness and her decision to leave him. Another instance of personal interaction involves Denis Kuznetsov, who initially works as a photojournalist for the newspaper and later joins the construction as a chauffeur. For Kuznetsov, the construction becomes a surrogate for his family, and he does not hesitate to sacrifice his life in order to stop the overflooding dam.

The two narrative lines are developed by means of different narrative devices. The story of the construction is told by an omniscient narrator who moves freely from a panoramic view to individual episodes, from one character to another, and who does not hesitate to offer his interpretation of events and his evaluation of characters. Only occasionally does the omniscient narrator make an effort to penetrate the minds of his characters and render their thoughts and feelings. He does so primarily in the episodes depicting the love relations between the engineer Karabut and Lera. Their illicit affair attracts a great deal of attention, bringing an emotional ingredient into the dry topic of the industrial novel.

Because he is given greater attention, especially in emotional matters, the characterization of Karabut is the most convincing among the industrial workers, overshadowing the portrayal of the director Ermasov and the workers Nagaev and Egers. Karabut's characterization is matched only by that of Koryshev, who acts as the personal narrator of the second line of the story. As narrator, Koryshev is most successful in communicating his own personality, a mixture of insecurity and growing confidence, passivity and defiance. He offers a convincing picture of his inner growth from an unassured journalist to a mature writer. In his depiction of other characters, Koryshev is openly biased, assessing them according to his own standards and values. As a result, the other journalists in the novel appear as one-dimensional figures, lacking credible personalities and psychological depth.

Koryshev is also biased in his interpretation of events, offering a one-sided evaluation of what goes on in the editorial office. As a newcomer, he sees things in a fresh way, but he lacks the knowledge of past events and of the longstanding relations between the members of the editorial board. To remedy the situation, Koryshev frequently introduces dialogues, reproducing directly the viewpoints of his colleagues. Dialogue occupies as much as half of Koryshev's story and gives the reader other points of view.

Stylistically, the two narratives do not differ from one another: both rely on standard, stylistically neutral language. Occasionally, however, the omniscient narrator imitates the elevated, solemn style of the Soviet press, glorifying industrial achievements and the dedication of workers. In *The Quenching of Thirst* this solemn intonation appears in the depiction of the self-sacrificing efforts of the workers to expedite the construction and to save the overflooding dam:

> The night was rushing by. People did not notice the freezing weather or the stars. Deafened by the iron thunder, they could not hear each other. They sat in cabs and grew stiff from the monotonous motions, from the frenzied desire to do the same things they did every day, but to do them better and much faster. They sat in their cabs until they were dead tired, then they jumped out onto the frosty sand, sat down, stretched out their legs or even lay down; and steam poured from their faces and hands when they took off their work gloves. . . (p. 300)

The same style distinguishes Koryshev's journalistic essays. He writes about the work in the desert in an elevated manner:

> We are driving along the canal. The incessant iron roar at times fades away, at times shakes the air threateningly. Clouds of dust rise like smoke above the machines. . . . A power shovel at work seems furious somehow. With an angry clang it throws its bucket to the ground like an unwanted burden, and for a second or two the bucket seems tired and rests lifelessly on the ground. To hell with it! I'm tired of working! But then the cable is put into motion and the open steel jaws slowly begin to bite into the ground. (pp. 150-51)

Overwhelmed by the grandiosity of the desert, Koryshev initially describes it with the help of elaborate similes and metaphors. In his first essay, with the characteristic title of "In the Sand Ocean," he develops the idea of people living in the desert as on an island, and speaks of "swimming dunes," "moire sand," and "burning mirage" (p. 63). Reprimanded for his pomposity, typical of newcomers to the desert, Koryshev gradually learns to depict the desert in simple and precise terms.

A similar simplicity marks the omniscient narrator's portrayal of the desert. The image of the desert appears frequently, and is always described in a brief and precise manner, such as:

> Hot weather came at the beginning of June. It was forty in the shade. The intense heat scorched the sky white, and the horizon was obscured by grainy, burning air, which moved in thick waves like fog. (p. 18)
> The desert was rippled with damp, cold sand. The heat is unbearable in the desert, but cold weather is even more dismal and depressing. (p. 212)

Although the novel takes place in the exotic setting of Turkmenia, it offers very little local color. Of all the construction workers depicted, there is only one Turkmenian, who keeps some local customs and traditions. He is Byashim Muradov, a young herdsman who comes to learn a trade and to earn money to pay "kalym" for his bride. At the suggestion of his fellow workers, he refuses to pay the "kalym" and is killed by his bride's relatives. Besides "kalym," only one other Turkmenian tradition, that of free wrestling, is depicted in the novel. "Giurek" takes place at the celebration of the Bolshevik Revolution, thus combining local custom with Soviet life.

Even less local color appears in the other story line, although it takes place in Ashkhabad and involves a local newspaper. None of the journalists portrayed by Koryshev is of Turkmenian origin, until the very end of the novel, when a Turkmenian is appointed as managing editor. A newcomer to Turkmenia, Koryshev seems to be more fascinated with the progress made in this once backward republic than with its old traditions. He describes at length the new towns in the desert and the reconstruction of Ashkhabad after the earthquake, but fails to notice the unique architecture or Muslim customs. At one point Koryshev is taken to see the ruins of Merv, the old Asiatic capital, but fails to appreciate the sight. He confesses to his companion:

> I was never able to get excited at the sight of old stones or feel anything solemn, like the continuity of centuries or the continuity of years, or even the continuity of time. But, on the other hand, I do have this feeling when I see people. (p. 281)

Koryshev conveys his fascination with people in his stories about Turkmenia, which he writes in his spare time and publishes in local magazines. Some of his stories have titles identical to those which Trifonov himself wrote a decade earlier. There are certain biographical similarities as well, such as a fatherless childhood, the stigma of being the son of "an enemy of the people," and the trip to Turkmenia. For both Koryshev and Trifonov, the trip to Turkmenia proved very fruitful: it provided Trifonov with material for a novel and a book of short stories, and it gave Koryshev the opportunity to regain self-esteem and trust, as well as to develop his creative skills. In the epilogue of the novel, he is shown leaving Turkmenia; in addition to being a successful journalist, he is also the author of a collection of essays and a film script about the Kara-Kum canal. His move back to Moscow clearly signals success and high hopes for the future.

The Quenching of Thirst received mixed reviews. Many critics placed the novel within the tradition of the industrial genre and stressed its uniqueness and originality. Thus, A. Bocharov commended Trifonov for "discovering new depths in a familiar channel, and being able to see what drifted past the shore in a new way...."[71] F. Kuznetsov praised the novel for investigating moral clashes and stressed that "the moral value of a character is tested in the novel by his or her attitude toward labor, especially collective labor."[72]

Some reviewers were critical, however, of the compositional complexity and the different narrative methods employed. F. Svetov claimed that the multi-layered composition and the lack of connection between episodes created vagueness in presenting the characters and conveying the main idea of "quenching thirst."[73] I. Tikhonov criticized Koryshev's introspective narrative, which, in his opinion, resembled "idle reflection, a kind of intelligent self-flagellation."[74] While writing his review, Tikhonov had no way of knowing that just such an intense interest in the inner world of his heroes would become a trademark of Trifonov's mature works, beginning with the stories written in the mid-sixties.

CHAPTER V

SHORT STORIES OF THE 1960s

The critic A. Turkov has noted that Trifonov's short stories often mark his transition from one period to another, from one style of writing to another.[75] Such is the case with the Turkmenian stories of the 1950s which mark his transition from plot-oriented literature, exemplified by *Students*, to a more "concentrated" way of writing with greater emphasis on the prose itself in *The Quenching of Thirst*. The stories of the mid- and late 1960s, on the other hand, indicate Trifonov's shift of focus from the exotic setting of Soviet Central Asia to familiar Moscow surroundings where the author depicts the moral problems faced by contemporary city dwellers. Together with the change of basic setting, came a change in the manner of writing: the focus shifts from the external depiction of characters and events to the reproduction of the protagonists' inner world through self-analysis, or in Trifonov's own words, "self-knowledge."[76]

The first signs of the new writing came with the short stories Trifonov wrote in the mid-sixties and published in *Novy Mir* in 1969, and later in the volume *The Cap with a Large Peak* (Kepka s bolshim kozyrkom). These stories included "Vera and Zoika" (Vera i Zoika), "A Summer Midday" (Byl letnii polden), "In an Autumn of Mushrooms" (V gribnuiu osen'), "A Journey" (Puteshestvie), and others.[77]

The last of these stories, "A Journey," although written later than the others, offers a perfect introduction to the new series.[78] It depicts a writer who is suffocating in the familiar surroundings of his Moscow apartment and who desperately wants to go somewhere to meet new people and gain new impressions. He asks a friendly newspaper editor to send him to an exciting industrial project, but instead is advised to go someplace nearby. On his way home, the writer realizes that he actually does not know Moscow itself, its new residential areas and even his own neighborhood. Moreover, he remains a stranger to himself. Thus, instead of undertaking an exotic trip, the writer decides to look around, try to learn more about himself and his neighbors, and in this way to find new material for his writing. Trifonov does exactly the same thing in his stories of the 1960s, portraying ordinary Muscovites going through the routine of everyday life with its joys and sorrows, its conflicts and solutions.

Thematically, all the Moscow stories are concerned with so-called *byt*, that is, details of everyday life, and emphasize the importance of the normal flow of life.[79] *Byt*, wrote Trifonov in his article "To Choose, to Decide, to Sacrifice," is life itself. It includes the complex interrelations of people, their opinions, friendships, acquaintances and hostilities. "*Byt* is the test of life, in which a contemporary morality appears and is tried out."[80] Trifonov's preoccupation with *byt* determined the nature of the plots in his short stories: they are extremely simple and deal with everyday life routines, such as cleaning a dacha ("Vera and Zoika"), attempts to get rid of pigeons ("The Death of the Pigeons"), or a trip to a small Bulgarian village, where, despite its long history, people go through the same routines of daily existence ("The Smallest Town"). Only a few stories depict more dramatic events, such as a mother's death ("In an Autumn of Mushrooms), or a return home after fifty-six years ("A Summer Midday"), but even in these the tragic effect is subdued by ordinary details and the feeling that, following the dramatic climax, life will return to normal.

The stories have a number of common features in their structure. First of all, they all follow the principle of a sudden beginning, which introduces the basic conflict immediately, without describing the circumstances and the characters involved in the action. Thus, "Vera and Zoika" begins with the sentence:

> Before lunch came a familiar client, number 5280, a neat and clean lady in a raincoat who always brought her linen with lots of men's items in clean and tidy packages. She asked Vera if she could go to the country and clean the dacha this weekend.[81]

The request to clean the dacha constitutes the beginning of the action, and the entire plot of the story revolves around that activity. The cleaning forms the basic action, which juxtaposes characters and reveals their personalities.

In a similar way, the opening sentence of "A Summer Midday" signals the plot—the heroine's return to her native town: "On her 73rd birthday Olga Robertovna decided to visit her birth place."[82] Unlike "Vera and Zoika," however, this story offers a short exposition providing a few more details about the heroine's life and her fifty-six year absence from her homeland.

Having clearly established the beginning of the action in the opening paragraph, the stories develop the plot in a fragmented manner, juxtaposing the present with the past, current events with recollections. Present events unfold in a short period of time and are arranged chronologically, while the past includes distant times, and these sections disregard rules of chronology and causality. Recollections of the past reappear not as a logical extension of present-day action, but as fragmented memory associations, triggered by different external stimuli. These reflections play an important role in conveying the meaning of the stories, by disclosing the protagonists' makeup and their general attitude to life.

In "A Summer Midday" the story of Olga Robertovna's trip to her native town acquires a special meaning thanks to her recollections of the last spring in that town and the short summary of her entire life. In terms of present time the plot unfolds in seven days, starting with Olga's departure from Moscow on a Tuesday, and ending with her return the next Monday. The five days in the Baltic town turn out to be extremely busy; Olga attends official ceremonies to honor her late husband, including a visit to the local museum and the Film Studio, and she meets with some old revolutionaries. On Saturday she takes advantage of a free day and goes to the place where she used to live. In a climactic scene that takes place at midday, as indicated in the title, she meets an old friend whom she has not seen for fifty-six years. Although their meeting is the most dramatic event of the story, it remains unreported. Instead the story summarizes Olga Robertovna's entire life, in the process explaining why she never got in touch with her friend. The story of Olga's life, full of sacrifices and deprivations, shows the heroine in a totally new light: this modest and soft-spoken woman, who chose to remain in her husband's shadow, proved to be as strong and as dedicated to the revolutionary cause as was he; she accompanied him into exile before the Revolution and was exiled herself in the purges of the 1930s. The ending of the story is totally unexpected: after returning to Moscow, Olga tells her acquaintance about the bad weather she experienced during her trip. The trivial remarks about the weather, along with such mundane details as waiting in line for milk, neutralize her revolutionary past and bring the action back to present reality, in which Olga reappears as an ordinary old lady concerned with daily problems rather than high revolutionary ideals.

The juxtaposition of a few days with an entire lifetime also governs the structure of the story "In an Autumn of Mushrooms," in which the sudden death of Antonina Vasilievna makes Nadya recall the difficult life of her mother, who single-handedly raised her two children without much help from her drunkard husband or her selfish sister.[83] Although Nadya's recollections are of her mother, they nevertheless point out the special relationship between her mother and herself, and help the reader to understand her grief. The plot of "In an Autumn of Mushrooms" is even simpler than that of "A Summer Midday," being restricted to Nadya's feelings as she tries to cope with her grief and readjust to life without her mother. The external events depicted in the story include the bare minimum: the discovery of the mother's corpse in the dacha, the arrival of Nadya's husband, and the family reunion following the funeral two days later. As in "A Summer Midday," the most dramatic events—the death and the funeral—are absent from the narrative, replaced by a description of the effect they have on the heroine. The climax of the story comes unexpectedly, with Aunt Frosya blaming Nadya for her mother's premature death. The accusation tarnishes the image of a loving daughter who cared about her mother, and suggests that Nadya had taken advantage of her mother, burdening her with raising grandchildren and doing all the domestic chores. The ending of the story is intentionally casual: Nadya returns to work and arranges for her two children to go to a playschool. Thus, as dramatic as the death is, it does not change the life of those who survived: Nadya has to go on living and readjusting to new circumstances.

The entire narrative of "In an Autumn of Mushrooms" depicts the viewpoint of Nadya, who acts as the central intelligence, evaluating everything and everyone in the story. Through Nadya's perception the reader learns about the mother's tragic death, the funeral preparations, and the gathering afterwards. From her recollections emerges an image of her mother as a self-sacrificing woman who devoted her entire life to her children and grandchildren. The other characters in the story, including Nadya's husband, his friend Levin, and Aunt Frosia are also seen through Nadya's eyes. Most importantly, the story reflects her reaction to what is happening around her and reveals her most intimate feelings, which include not only grief and loneliness over her mother's death, but also jealousy, a strong attachment to her husband, and her affection for, and helplessness with, her children. All in all, the narrative method superbly reveals the psychological makeup of the heroine, and demonstrates her readjustment to life in new circumstances.

Trifonov used a similar method of narration in his other stories written in the late 1960s, such as "A Summer Midday," "Vera and Zoika," and, in part, "The Death of the Pigeons." Instead of portraying events through the eyes of an outside witness/narrator, as was done in the Turkmenian series, these stories convey the inner world of the protagonists with little interference from an omniscient author. Thus, the story "A Summer Midday" is told by Olga Robertovna, who describes both the details of her trip and her reaction to what she experiences. A great part of the narrative reproduces her recollections of the past, stirred by familiar sights and old friends. In both time frames of the story Olga appears as the only "central intelligence," evaluating the past and the present, and expressing her opinions about herself and others.

In "Vera and Zoika" the narrative primarily conveys the viewpoint of Vera, one of the three female characters portrayed in the story. The reader learns about events through her, and her opinions form the basis for the characterization of the other two women. Unlike "A Summer Midday," however, where the narrative method was focused on the heroine's inner self, in "Vera and Zoika" some insight is provided into the makeup of other characters as well. Vera's brief but seemingly accurate remarks about Zoika, with whom she has been sharing a communal apartment, and her acute observations about Lidya Alexandrovna, whom she has known only casually as a client at the drycleaners, prepare the reader for a direct encounter with both characters that only confirms Vera's characterization of them. Zoika proves to be the direct opposite of Vera—bitter and unhappy, distrustful and self-centered, while Lidya Alexandrovna is similar to Vera—open and friendly, always hoping for the best. Unlike Vera, who is portrayed mainly through her thoughts, the other two female characters are revealed through dialogues in which they openly express their opinions and feelings.

This method of storytelling, however, is not typical of Trifonov's mature stories, which as a rule have a minimum of dialogue and rely on straightforward narration that at first seems to be an objective account told by an omniscient narrator, but upon closer scrutiny can be seen as a type of indirect reported speech which conveys the central character's point of view. All the stories make frequent use of verbs of perception and evaluation, which signal the protagonists' subjective reactions to surroundings and events. The writing concentrates on the protagonists' physical and emotional states, which vary from relative tranquillity to complex anxiety. The narrative often uses conventional colloquial phrases to convey the subjective opinions of characters.

All these linguistic features are evident in the story "In an Autumn of Mushrooms," which recounts Nadya's reaction to her mother's sudden death in three distinctive stages: first, in terms of her physical perception and emotional response to the body; secondly, through the physical and psychological numbness and debilitation that follow; and thirdly, through

Nadya's full realization of the tragedy, both intellectually and emotionally. At the beginning of the story, the reader learns about Nadya's discovery of her mother's corpse in sensual terms. At this stage verbs of perception predominate, indicating what she can "see," "notice," "hear," or "smell." Along with the verbs of perception appear phrases indicating Nadya's growing feeling of unease: she "subconsciously noticed the dark porch and the dark window," then she experienced "a sudden and strong feeling of worry," and "her heart felt something would happen" (pp. 199-202).

Emotional anxiety leads to physical distress: "Nadya's heart begins to beat faster," she grows "short of breath." The physical discomfort Nadya experiences is described at length in the middle section of the story, providing such details as: "wooden-like arms," "shaking hands and trembling body," "shortness of breath and heartache," and "shivering and lack of strength" (pp. 200-206). Finally comes the painful realization of the inevitability of this death, captured in the story with the help of verbs which describe growing awareness: "to understand," "to grasp," "to realize," and "to be concerned." Awaking at night, Nadya at first worries that she has slept through something very important, but then:

> she heard a voice from the dream: mother had died. These words seemed to her like delirium, they did not mean anything, but a second later they acquired meaning, a meaning that grew to immense and clear proportions until it struck Nadya; she fell down, and lay deathlike, with a heavy weight pressing on her heart. (p. 206)

The second instance of Nadya's painful realization occurs at the post-funeral gathering. Sitting in the next room, not wanting to join the guests in the kitchen, Nadya can mentally see all the objects that were used by her mother:

> pans, graters, cast-iron pots, an ancient copper mortar . . . and in the left compartment—all kinds of drugs, herbs in packages, jars of dried raspberries, chicory, soda, neatly tied-up pieces of string, . . . All of these things remained and continued to exist—newspapers folded on the table next to the ironing board. . . the apron of dark-red cotton was hanging, as always, near the sink. . . . But she was not there. Not in the bathroom, not in the hall. Not at the dacha. The rooms were dark there, everything was closed up at that cursed dacha where rain was pouring down on the wooden porch. She was nowhere. Nowhere, nowhere. (p. 208)

The enumeration of inanimate objects that continue to exist after the person who used them has disappeared creates a mood of despair. This mood is strengthened by the repetition of the word "nowhere," conveying Nadya's full realization of the finality of her mother's death. The quoted passage also contains a reference to the "cursed" dacha, the place where her mother had died. The same phrase appeared earlier when Nadya thinks of the dacha as "the cursed dacha! . . . the place was so unattractive, the owner so gloomy" (p. 202).

The use of negative adjectives, as well as adverbs of uncertainty and indefinite pronouns, emphasizes the heroine's point of view. Words like "probably," "perhaps" and "maybe" convey Nadya's uncertainty about what is happening and how to react to it. The same function is performed by the rhetorical questions posed occasionally in the text: "Why did she call her mother a person?" in the telegram she sent, or "What is going to happen now? How am I to live?" (p. 203). All the linguistic features noted above signal the appearance of indirect reported speech in "In an Autumn of Mushrooms." A careful analysis of Trifonov's other stories of the 1960s would show a similar usage of this type of speech.

Trifonov's consistent reliance on reporting the thoughts of his characters determined another stylistic peculiarity of the stories, namely, their extreme simplicity. The narrative is totally devoid of elaborate similes or metaphors and relies on simple epithets or qualifiers that convey the distinctive characteristics of the objects and persons depicted. Thus, in "In an Autumn of Mushrooms" a negative attitude toward the dacha is communicated by the qualifiers "cursed," "gloomy," and "ugly," while the crowdedness of the small Moscow apartment is conveyed by the enumeration of objects stored in the kitchen. Similarly, the secondary characters are portrayed with the help of a few significant details: the love and concern of Nadya's husband are shown by his gentle caresses, while Aunt Frosya's pinkish face suggests her easy and comfortable life, so different from her sister's constant struggles.

A close attention to detail characterizes all the stories of the 1960s; instead of elaborate descriptions of external circumstances and feeling, the narrative uses a particular detail to convey the essence of an event, character or emotion. As a result, the stories are extremely compact and yet very suggestive. The stories of the 1960s show a continued reliance on a "concentrated" style of writing in which words carry multiple meanings and interpretations are left open to the reader.

CHAPTER VI
MOSCOW NOVELLAS

The stories of the 1960s, which portrayed the everyday life of ordinary Muscovites and paid close attention to their inner world, paved the way for Trifonov's "urban" or "Moscow" novellas, written at the end of the 1960s and during the 1970s. They included *The Exchange*, *Taking Stock*, *The Long Goodbye*, and *Another Life*. These four works are of greater length, extending from fifty to a hundred pages, and have a greater variety of characters and a broader development of milieu than the stories. The terms "urban" and "Moscow" are frequently applied to this series because they have a common urban, or, more precisely Moscow setting, which appears not only as a background, but actually determines the narrative tone and atmosphere.

Although published separately and at different times, the four novellas are united by a common theme and an emphasis on the exploration of thoughts and feelings. As rightly noticed by A. Bocharov, the emotions of characters constitute the moving force behind the plots of the novellas: they mark the beginning, the climax and the denouement of the action.[84] The plots of the novellas center around the mental states and feelings of the protagonists who are captured by the author in a moment of crisis, as they try to establish what has happened to them. The title "Taking Stock" can be applied to all the novellas, since all the protagonists are trying to evaluate their lives and to draw "preliminary conclusions." Their findings are rather tragic: they are dissatisfied with their work, their families, and usually with themselves.

The dissatisfaction of Trifonov's heroes with their work is most surpris-

ing, since all of them are highly educated and work in fields which theo-
retically offer immense possibilities for creativity and contentment. They
are writers and actors, literary scholars and translators, as well as
reasearchers in the humanities and social sciences. The reasons for their
dissatisfaction are manifold: some fail because of lack of talent; others lack
self-discipline and can never complete their projects. But the most frus-
trated characters are those who regret their choice of profession. In
Taking Stock the protagonist realizes that he has wasted his talent as a
writer by becoming a mediocre translator who simply "produces rubbish." The protagonist of *The Exchange* is unhappy with his work in the
Oil Institute because he has always wanted to be a painter.

However, these characters' professional lives constitute only the background of Trifonov's novellas. The foreground is occupied by family life,
which, in the writer's opinion, reveals more about human nature than the
depiction of professional and social life alone. The heroes are portrayed
above all in relation to their immediate families, especially their wives and
children. Their wives turn out to be strong and domineering, often suppressing their husbands' individuality, and thereby contributing to their
feeling of alienation. Many of Trifonov's couples experience a gradual
cooling of their feelings; they are faced with growing indifference in their
relationship. In extreme cases, they cease to care about each other
entirely, which has a dramatic effect on their psychological makeup. "If a
person doesn't feel the love of those who are close to him," says the protagonist of *Taking Stock,* "then no matter how ideologically sound, spiri-
tually he begins to suffocate. There isn't enough air to breathe."[85]

As a rule, each family has only one child. As long as the children are
small, they do not create any problems, but the moment they reach their
teens, they begin to rebel against their parents. The first signs of rebellion
are described in *Another Life,* when Irinka refuses to listen to her mother.
An open conflict is portrayed in *Taking Stock* when Kirill quarrels with his
father and runs away from home. He returns after twenty-four hours, but
continues to disregard his parents.

The novellas present not only the protagonists' immediate families,
but also their parents and in-laws. For the most part, these families differ
greatly from one another—one being honest and idealistic, the
other—greedy and selfish. The contrast between families is nowhere as
apparent as in *The Exchange,* where the highly idealistic Dmitrievs are
contrasted with the philistine Lukianovs, who are concerned primarily
with wealth and comfort. The Lukianovs are portrayed in the novella as
people "who know how to live," i.e., how to establish contacts with the
"right" people and be rewarded with benefits. The Dmitrievs, on the
other hand, are rarely concerned with themselves, but always try to help

others. Ksenya Fyodorovna, the protagonist's mother,

> was constantly surrounded by people in whose fates she constantly
> took part. For months some elderly people she barely knew had
> been living in her room, friends of Georgy Alexeevich's, and some
> old ladies who were even more decrepit, his grandfather's friends,
> and some casual acquaintances from vacation houses who wanted
> to get to the Moscow doctors, or provincial boys and girls, chil-
> dren of distant relatives who had come to Moscow to enter insti-
> tutes. His mother tried to help all of them absolutely disinterest-
> edly. But why should she help? All ties had been lost long ago, and
> she was worn out. But still—with shelter, advice, sympathy. (p.
> 58)

As a result of such basic differences, the two families cannot get along.
The hostility is especially apparent in the spouses' attitude toward their
mothers-in-law. In *The Exchange* Lena openly despises Ksenya
Fyodorovna, calling her a hypocrite, while Dmitriev simply hides his real
feelings towards his mother-in-law. In *Another Life* Olga resents her
mother-in-law, and in *The Long Goodbye* the protagonist strongly dislikes
his "teshcha." The feeling is mutual, for all the mothers-in-law consider
their daughters- and sons-in-law unworthy spouses for their children.

The family conflicts mentioned above play an important role in the
development of plot, but the central conflict is internal—the struggle
between opposing values which takes place in the protagonist's own
mind. Faced with difficult moral decisions, all Trifonov's heroes go
through a period of long and complex inner struggle, carefully analyzing
all the pros and cons of their dilemma. The decisions they reach, however,
are usually based on purely selfish motives and ignore basic values of honesty and concern. Thus, the hero of *The Exchange* submits to pressure
from his wife and asks his sick mother to exchange her apartment and to
live with her hostile daughter-in-law. The motive of the exchange is not
to help the sick person, but to acquire a bigger apartment after her death.
Ksenya Fyodorovna agrees to the exchange, but comments: "You have
already made an exchange, Vitya." She is referring to Dmitriev's acceptance of the shallow principles held by his wife and her parents, whose
only concern is money and the material welfare of their immediate family.

The theme of exchange of moral principles first introduced in *The
Exchange* echoes through all Trifonov's novellas.[86] In *Taking Stock*
Gennady gives up the principles of basic honesty and decency in order to
have peace at home. In *The Long Goodbye* Lyalya sacrifices her relationship
with Grisha in order to land a role in a new play, while Grisha is willing to

collaborate with his rival in order to see his work staged. The only character who resists the pressure to conform and remains faithful to his idealistic principles is the protagonist of *Another Life*, but he pays a high price:
he dies from a heart attack at the age of forty-two.

While examining the roots of indifference and cynicism, Trifonov con-
sistently looks at his heroes from the inside, rather than from the outside.
In all the novellas he relies on a narration that either conveys the protagonist's point of view directly in the first person singular, as in *Taking Stock*,
or indirectly in the third person, as in *The Exchange*, *The Long Goodbye*,
and *Another Life*. The four novellas display an impressive range of narrative methods that skillfully reproduce the protagonists' feelings.

The Exchange

At first glance the story of *The Exchange* seems to be told by an omniscient narrator. The major conflict is introduced in the first paragraph of
the novella, and the next two paragraphs give a short prehistory of the
events that preceded the idea of an exchange. Indeed, the beginning of
the action and the prologue convey the voice of an omniscient narrator
who, in an impassioned and concise manner, informs the reader about the
three chief characters and their relations during the past fourteen years.
The emphasis is clearly on the figure of Dmitriev, who had made many
futile attempts to reconcile his wife and mother, characterized as "two
good women who dearly loved Dmitriev," but "who cultivated mutual
hostility which had grown harder with the years."[87]

The above sentence, appearing at the end of the prologue, suggests to
a perceptive reader the emergence of Dmitriev's point of view: it presents
his evaluation of both women and himself, and his bewilderment over
their growing hostility. The transition from an "omniscient" to a "concealed narrator"[88] becomes clearly pronounced in the first episode, which
depicts a conversation between Lena and Dmitriev about the exchange.
The entire episode is described from the point of view of Dmitriev, who,
struck by Lena's cold calculations, experiences a great deal of physical and
mental discomfort.

Having clearly established Dmitriev as the central intelligence in the
first episode, Trifonov continues to present his point of view throughout
the novella. Dmitriev acts as a typical "concealed" narrator who, in a
seemingly objective third-person singular, presents a highly subjective
perspective, with his own interpretation of events and his own evaluation
of characters.

As is typical of a concealed narrator, Dmitriev is never off stage; he is in the center of events depicted in the novella, starting with the evening conversation with Lena, through the next day's routine at work, a short visit to Tanya, a trip to Pavlinovo to see his sick mother, and finally his return to Moscow the following morning. All the above events unfold in the short span of thirty-six hours, but in addition to the present time, the novella contains numerous reminiscences from the past, stretching as far back as Dmitriev's childhood some thirty years earlier.[89]

Like the events in the present, all the reminiscences are filtered through Dmitriev's mind. He recollects the most crucial episodes in his life. Most of his reminiscing takes place during his travel from one place to another, especially during his long trip to Pavlinovo, when he stops at the shore of a river in order to delay the talk with his mother. Led by his memory associations, Dmitriev recollects his early childhood, his first years of marriage, the clashes between Lena and her parents on the one hand and his family on the other, the disturbing story with his friend Lyovka, and many other episodes.

As befits true recollections, these do not follow any chronological or logical pattern; they simply arise from random memory associations. Sometimes the sight of a person brings back the memory of past relations: the talk with Tanya reminds Dmitriev of their affair three years earlier. Most frequently, there is a chain of associations, one leading to another: the thought of his grandfather brings back the memory of the clash he had with the Lukianovs; the grandfather's funeral leads to recollections of strained relations between Dmitriev and Lyovka after Dmitriev had accepted a job promised for his friend. These reminiscences provide additional information about Dmitriev. They allow the reader to see more of his indecisiveness and weak character, which explains his gradual transformation from an idealistic Dmitriev to a philistine Lukianov.

Dmitriev's point of view is emphasized by the frequent use of verbs which indicate the process of remembering, words which express uncertainty and doubt and words of evaluation and reasoning. Recollecting the initial relations between his family and the Lukianovs, Dmitriev comments:

> Strange to remember it. Could it have really been like that: everyone sitting together on the veranda at the big table, drinking tea, Ksenya Fyodorovna pouring, Vera Lazarevna cutting the pie? And she called Lora *Lorochka* at one time, and arranged for her to have her best dressmakers. It had been like that, for sure. It had been, it had been. Only it didn't stay in his memory, it rushed past and vanished, because he couldn't live for anything, or see anyone but Lena. (p. 64-65)

Dmitriev's point of view is also dominant in the narration of present events. We are given his perception and interpretation of events and his descriptions and evaluations of the other characters as well as of himself. He is far more harsh on the others than on himself, trying to justify his compliance with Lena and the Lukianovs as "natural" and "inevitable." In the same way Dmitriev tries to justify to himself his affair with Tanya, his dishonesty with his friend Lyovka Bubrik, and even the idea of the apartment exchange. Thus, Dmitriev reflects on the "benefits" of the exchange:

> They would make the exchange, receive a good separate apart-
> ment, would live together. And the sooner the exchange was made
> the better. For his mother's well-being. Her dream would be real-
> ized. It would be psychotherapy, the healing of the soul! No, Lena
> was sometimes very wise, intuitively, womanlike—suddenly it dawns
> on her. Really, that's possibly the only brilliant means of saving a
> life. When the surgeons are powerless other forces come into play. .
> . . And that's what not one professor could do, no one, no one, no
> one! (p. 34)

If Dmitriev alone were responsible for guiding the readers' perception, they would have to accept his idealized version of himself, or speculate on the true dimensions of his character. The author, however, interpolates into the narrative information that suggests another point of view with such physical details as "a not very young, heavy man with an unhealthy color in his face, with the eternal smell of tobacco in his mouth"; or psychological traits: "his usual timidity," "indecision," and his being "full of smugness."

The difference between the voice of the omniscient narrator and that of Dmitriev is minimal, but what clearly distinguishes the two is the underlying tone of irony and sarcasm. Thus, speaking about Dmitriev's hesitation to accept the job promised to Bubrik, the omniscient narrator points out:

> And Dmitriev really didn't want to do it. He didn't sleep for three
> nights, he wavered and worried but gradually that which it was
> impossible to think of, which was not the thing to do, turned into
> something inconsequential, diminutive, well-packed like a capsule
> you had to—it was necessary even, for your health—swallow, despite
> the nastiness it contained inside. There is no one who doesn't notice
> nastiness after all. But everyone swallows the capsules. (p. 81)

The omniscient narrator's sarcastic remarks are not directed exclusively at Dmitriev; he adds his revealing strokes to the portrayal of Lena and her mother, characterizing Vera Lazarevna as "a toiler with a self-abnegating nature" (p. 30), and Lena as "such a nice-looking lady-bulldog with short straw-colored hair, and an always pleasantly tanned, slightly dark face. She didn't let up until her wishes—right in her teeth—turned into flesh. A great trait! Wonderful, amazingly decisive in life. The trait of real men" (p. 79).

In addition to such scattered evaluative remarks, the voice of the omniscient narrator replaces Dmitriev's in some descriptive passages. This occurs in the novella's prologue, as well as in the description of the co-operative "The Red Partisans" and in the denouement of the plot, providing minute details of the exchange and a brief mention of Ksenya Fyodorovna's impending death. The accumulation of trivial information about the exchange procedures overshadows the fact of Ksenya Fyodorovna's death, thus emphasizing the inhumanity and cruelty of the exchange.

A similar tone of accusation is felt in the novella's epilogue, written in the first-person singular, where the narrator identifies himself as a friend from Dmitriev's past to whom Dmitriev has recently related the entire story of the exchange. The introduction of a personalized narrator in the last paragraph of the novella disrupts the smooth flow of the third-person narrative. The reader is given some new information—the narrator recollects new details about Dmitriev's childhood and describes his sudden aging after his mother's death—but this information does not add any new dimension to the story. The rhetorical question put forward by the personalized narrator, "What could I say to Dmitriev?..", seems unnecessary as well; it is obvious all along that the narrator will not give a clear-cut evaluation of the protagonist and that the reader must establish his own interpretation.

Taking Stock

Unlike *The Exchange,* which relied on a "concealed narrator," *Taking Stock* is written in the first-person singular and conveys the perspective of its hero, Gennady Sergeevich. Acting as the sole narrator in the novella, Gennady tells the story of his alienation from his family, his dissatisfaction with his work as a translator, and above all, his frustration with himself, with his inability to change anything in his life.

The novella begins abruptly as Gennady places a long distance call to

Moscow and announces his plans to return. At this point, the reader does not know the identity of the hero or the person he is calling, and no explanation is given for his sudden call. The only information provided concerns tropical heat and its negative effects on the hero's health:

> At the beginning of May the city was struck by a tropical heat wave and life became unbearable. From eleven in the morning until sunset the hotel room was as hot as an oven and I would begin to feel dizzy and short of breath. One night was particularly bad, and tormented by sleeplessness, pains in my chest, and the fear of death, I lost heart.[90]

In the next paragraph, the reader learns about the narrator's change of plans: instead of going to Moscow, he agrees to go to Tokhir and is taken there by his friend Mansur. From this point on the action of the novella unfolds simultaneously on two planes: present events, taking place in Tokhir, a resort near Ashkhabad, and past recollections, reconstructing the narrator's life in Moscow over the past forty-eight years.[91]

Characteristically, the present plays a minor role in the novella: it is restricted to less than two weeks and occupies less than a quarter of the narrative. Furthermore, there are no dramatic collisions in the present. The present action consists of the narrator's progress in his work on a translation of Mansur's poem and his talks with the resort manager Atabaly and Atabaly's adopted daughter Valya. A great deal of attention is devoted to Gennady's physical and psychological states, for example:

> I was still in bed, utterly exhausted from my sleepless night. By all indications my blood pressure had shot up. Perhaps because there was about to be a change in the weather—either a cool spell or even worse heat. Or perhaps I had been working too hard—my brain was tired, and I needed a break. (p. 179)

In contrast to the uneventful and retrospective present, the past is full of dramatic conflicts, including family feuds, strained relations with friends and relatives, and a criminal case, involving Gennady's son Kirill, who had sold an old icon to a black-market dealer. As in the other Moscow novellas, the past is filtered through the hero's memory, and as such is devoid of strict chronological order. Memories of the recent past frequently precede those of distant times; many of them end abruptly, without indicating any outcome or future consequences. Thus the story of Gennady's first marriage appears after the lengthy account of his recent family problems, and the existence of the son from the first marriage is mentioned only briefly, without any details as to his name, profession or marital status.

As in true recollections, past events are linked to each other in various ways. Remembering a person can lead to past memories: while thinking about Rita, Gennady recollects their first happy years as well as their recent quarrels and reconciliations. Or, physical resemblance can bring back the memory of another person: the tall and plump nurse Valya reminds Gennady of his first wife and their dull marriage twenty-three years earlier. Most frequently, however, past events appear in a chain sequence, with one event leading to another: a recollection of Kirill's entrance exams brings back the memories of his tutor Gartvig and his influence on Rita; that in turn leads to reminiscences about the housekeeper Nyura and the story of the icon that her aunt had sent.

Reminiscences are also motivated realistically; Gennady recalls his past on his way to Tokhir, between periods of work on the translation, and above all during his sleepless nights. Troubled by his heart and suffering from insomnia, Gennady spends many sleepless nights recollecting his past and trying "to take stock of his life." He briefly recalls his childhood, his years as a student, and his first marriage, but dwells at length on recent problems with his family: his wife Rita is preoccupied with her own life and neglects her husband and son, while their son Kirill openly scorns them and behaves cruelly toward the housekeeper Nyura.

In telling the story of his marital and parental problems, Gennady is highly critical of his wife and son. He blames Rita for the break-up of their marriage and for raising Kirill as a callous egoist:

> I told her that I found the whole business very distasteful. I said that her pseudo-religiosity was so much hypocrisy and deceit, and that the first commandment of any religion—and of Christianity all the more so—was to love thy neighbor. And yet, what did one find with her? Indifference, abandonment of home, bookish vanity. Her husband neglected, and her son left to run wild. It must be menopause, my dear, menopause. And what was needed for that was not Thomas Aquinas but long daily walks and cold rubdowns in the morning. (p. 136)

Not sharing Rita's fascination with the Russian idealist philosphers Leontiev and Berdyaev, Gennady sarcastically calls them "Beliberdyaevs," a pun on "beliberda," a Russian word for "rubbish" or "nonsense." He refers to Rita's mentor Gartvig as "a sort of Grushchorin, an embodiment of two different figures, Pechorin and Grushnitsky" (p. 153).

As for his son, Gennady regards him as a total failure, continuously referring to him by such derogatory terms as "blockhead," "good-for-nothing," "scum" and "bastard." Only once does Gennady admit his own responsibility for Kirill's lack of principles. Sitting in the prosecutor's office and answering questions about Kirill's sale of an old icon, Gennady:

> . . . was suddenly overwhelmed by a feeling that was even more oppressive and more unbearable than fear—a feeling of terrible shame. Because it was, after all, I! I, I myself, and no one else! It was not Kirill, but I who was sitting in front of the investigator's desk and being questioned by this young man who eyed me with cool disdain. Oh, I felt this very distinctly! And if it hadn't been me, my whole being with all my guts, but had merely been a part of myself, a certain Kirill sitting in front of the investigator's desk, I would never have felt that disdain nor experienced that painful sense of shame. (p. 175)

The rest of the time Gennady is far less critical of himself, trying to blame his failures on external circumstances and fate. He speaks of the early loss of his parents, his wound in World War II, and his desire to catch up with life after the war. In his pursuit of an easy and pleasant life, Gennady gave up creative writing and switched to translating, which he himself regards as "rubbish." In a moment of honesty, he admits:

> It was humiliating, of course. I had accomplished very little. From an outsider's point of view it might not appear that way. I've done this, that, and a number of things. But I myself know how little it amounted to. I had planned to do things differently. (p. 126)

Gennady is critical of himself at several other times: he describes himself as "lazy and undisciplined by nature," "apathetic," and "a neurotic idiot."

The narrative of those passages which contain Gennady's recollections can be described as an extended monologue, but it is a highly organized and rational monologue, rather than the disjointed stream of consciousness so typical of modern fiction. The narrative in this type of monologue tends to rely on rhetorical questions, emphatic statements, and words and construction which suggest the narrator's attempts at reasoning. Thinking about his marriage of twenty years, Gennady reflects:

> We should not have lived together for twenty years. *Also sprach Zarathustra:* that's too long. Twenty years is no joke! In twenty years forests thin out and the soil becomes depleted. Even the best

house requires repairs. Turbines stop functioning. And as for the tremendous advances made by science in twenty years—it's awesome to contemplate! Revolutionary discoveries take place in all areas of human knowledge. Whole cities are rebuilt. October Square, which we once lived right next to, had changed its appearance completely. Never mind the fact that new states have arisen in Africa. Twenty years! A time span which can destroy all hopes. (p. 123)

Predominant as it is in the narrative structure of the novella, the monologue occasionally gives way to dialogue, usually an indirect dialogue, filtered through Gennady's memory and with his own distinctive interpretation. This type of indirect dialogue allows Gennady to superimpose his view on other characters' thoughts and to convey his version of the story to the reader. Gennady's rendition of his quarrel with Rita provides an example of this technique:

Even that last day, when we quarrelled about the mortgage payment and Rita said that I was just another Professor Serebryakov, that she had always hoped to find something in me, but there was nothing there, I was just a blank, another Professor Serebryakov—even then I listened and didn't explode because I could feel that there was pain in her words, genuine pain. But after all, Professor Serebryakov was a human being too. Why be so contemptuous of him? He wasn't a gangster or a rapist, he simply wanted to live, like anyone else. He loved a woman, in his own way, to the extent of his capacity, and for years he had worked away at one thing writing, writing, and more writing. Just as I had done. (p. 181)

In spite of Gennady's sincere attempt to prove his case, the above passage succeeds in drawing a parallel between him and Chekhov's Professor Serebryakov in the same way as Rita's earlier remark about the feminine weakness of Gennady's character succeeds in making its point. However subjective and one-sided in their interpretation, indirect dialogue offers the reader the possibility of a different perspective and evaluation.

Gennady's subjective account is also often contradicted by the simple juxtaposition of his words and actions. His plea for understanding and love in a family, for instance, does not coincide with his own behavior, and the painful process of "taking stock" proves to be just a futile exercise. In the epilogue of the novella Gennady returns to Moscow, makes up with his wife and son, and shortly thereafter goes to a Baltic resort, where he enjoys the mild weather and refreshing sea air. The healing effect of the Baltic climate provides a contrast to the beginning of the novella, which describes the oppressive heat and Gennady's chest pains in Central Asia. Happy with his improved condition, Gennady seems oblivious to his earlier dissatisfaction with his "rubbish" work, his family and himself. He is back exactly where he was at the beginning of the novella, complaining and blaming others, rather than trying to change anything in himself.

The Long Goodbye

From the point of view of narrative structure, *The Long Goodbye* stands out as the most complex of the four Moscow novellas. It places two protagonists (Lyalya, Grisha) in the center of the narrative and traces their inner thoughts and feelings through "concealed" narration. In addition to these two distinctive narrative voices, the novella also introduces points of view of two minor characters (Smolyanov, Telepnev), and contains the voice of an omniscient narrator, thus offering a wide variety of viewpoints.

Corresponding to the complex narrative technique, the novella has an elaborate temporal structure, encompassing events of the present, past and future. The present occupies the most prominent place, covering the period from the end of the summer of 1952 to December of the following year. The novella depicts the sudden rise of the theatrical actress Lyalya Telepneva following her affair with the playwright Smolyanov, and contrasts her success with the failures of her common-law husband Grisha Rebrov, who is not able to sell his plays and film scripts.

As in the other Moscow novellas here, too, the past plays an important role, illuminating the roots of present-day conflicts and providing explanations for the characters' complex personalities. The past appears for the most part in the reminiscences of Grisha, who looks back at his difficult childhood and examines his relationship with Lyalya over the past ten years. Lyalya is far less retrospective, preferring to dwell on her present-day accomplishments and problems.

In addition to these two temporal layers, the novella offers a unique glimpse into the future, outlining developments that would take place some eighteen years later. The future appears both in the prologue and epilogue, which comprise a distinct temporal frame. But whereas the epilogue provides a general summary of the protagonists' later life, the prologue emphasizes the external changes that had drastically transformed a Moscow suburb into a busy, modern center. The changes are conveyed in a highly metaphoric style, using the image of a lilac bush which, "unable to confine itself to the limits of the fence, overflowed into the street in a burst of riotous growth."[92] Eighteen years later, the lilac bush is replaced by an eight-story apartment building that has a butcher shop on the ground floor: the change is symbolic of the encroachment of utilitarian and prosaic aspects of life.

The images of the lilac bush and the butcher shop reappear in the epilogue in Lyalya's brief recollections of her past as she passes by the apartment building. The notion of rapid change is reinforced by the picture of Moscow spreading farther and farther out and "throwing up building after building, a stone mountain with a million lighted windows; it was laying bare the ancient soil, traversing it with giant concrete pipes, strewing the land with foundation pits, laying asphalt, building up, tearing down, destroying without a trace" (p. 353).

Both the prologue and the end of the epilogue are written by an omniscient narrator who describes the changes that occurred in the Moscow suburb and the lives of its inhabitants. This metaphoric style distinguishes the omniscient narrator from the "concealed" narrator, who captures the viewpoints of the two protagonists, as well as some minor characters, in a less poetic literary style.

The slight differences between individual narrative voices reflect the differences in the psychological makeup of the characters rather than their professional or educational background. Thus, the extrovert, Lyalya, tends to depict the exciting life around her through expressive qualifiers and modifiers as well as words expressing certainty and self-assurance, while the introspective Grisha prefers to brood and relies on verbs which express his feelings and on phrases expressing uncertainty and doubt.

The voices of Lyalya and Grisha play an equally important role in the novella, each taking up almost half of the narrative, leaving just a few pages for other characters. The novella begins with Lyalya's point of view; through her perception the reader learns about the company's tour of Saratov, her difficulties with the new assistant producer Smurny, and her worries about Grisha. Through her eyes the reader observes Smolyanov's party and judges the actor's rude behavior and the playwright's embarrassment:

> . . . she found it distressing to see Smurny's smug face before her at the head of the table. It was irritating to watch him throw back the hair from his eyes—his eyes now carefully avoiding hers—and to listen to the silly toasts, jokes and mutual eggings on. Equally revolting was the way in which Pashka Kornilovich and Makeev in their usual vulgar fashion, and Smurny too, though somewhat more subtly—teased the poor author, actually ridiculing him. The author

didn't understand their jokes, or at least not all of them, and would make feeble attempts to joke back. (p. 217)

Lyalya's narrative is most concerned with her own feelings and emotions, however. In the first part of the novella, she describes her dissatisfaction with the new producer, Smurny, and her lack of confidence in herself and her acting abilities. Following the unpleasant encounter with Smurny, Lyalya is overtaken by doubts: "And these doubts were the worst of all—the thing that nearly killed her. What if they were right? What if I really have no talent?" (p. 214).

Lyalya's general mood and self-evaluation change drastically in the central part of the novella, which depicts the rapid rise of her career. She accepts her success and popularity as fully deserved and is convinced that "things would stay this way and perhaps be even better in the future." (p. 232). They indeed get even better with Lyalya's invitation to the Movie Studio, her substantial raise in salary, and her nomination for an award. In December 1953, Lyalya enjoys "the comforting sensation of being a wealthy woman," and explains this feeling in the following passage:

> This sensation was a complex one, on many levels, and had little to do with the amount of money in her pocket—money was one thing she did not have, it disappeared so quickly. Rather, her sense of well-being was reflected in other things: in the fact, for example, that in cold weather she was warm. In this luxurious merino lamb coat with its fresh, lovely fragrance, she had no fear of the cold weather—perhaps for the first time in her life. It was also reflected in the peace of mind she felt with regard to that which is most important in life and without which one has no sort of life at all. For now no one would dare to say anything bad about her or even to think it. (pp. 272-73)

First introduced in the narrative by Lyalya, and portrayed as "painfully proud," and "full of complexes and overly sensitive about everything," Grisha Rebrov is eventually given an independent voice, a voice which only confirms the earlier characterization. He proves to be morbidly self-conscious, constantly worrying about the impression he makes on others, and fearing the possibility of making a fool of himself. Extremely knowledgeable and ambitious, he lacks the self-discipline to finish his projects and to strive for their acceptance.

In contrast to Lyalya, Grisha is preoccupied with his past, as if searching for the answers to his present-day problems in his childhood traumas. With bitterness he recalls his mentally disturbed father, who spied on him and forced the family to move to another district, thereby isolating Grisha from his school and his playmates. He contemplates the loss of his entire family during the war, which left him totally alone.

Withdrawn and reserved, Grisha seldom confides his problems to others, preferring to brood over his emotions himself. He conveys his emotional and physical state in the form of an indirect interior monologue which registers all subtle changes in his mood and feelings. His narrative relies heavily on verbs to communicate his feelings and on numerous modifiers that indicate the subtle differences in his emotional state:

> There wasn't any possibility of his sleeping, of course, but to remain in the same room with his sobbing mother-in-law was beyond his strength. He went upstairs to his and Lyalya's room and tried to read, but was unable to concentrate. So he lay down on the bed, smoked, and felt miserable. Sometimes he would be overcome by drowsiness, and the next few minutes would pass in a sort of delirium. Then he would suddenly jump up and reach for a cigarette. (p. 294)

Grisha's mood of self-doubt and depression changes abruptly towards the end of the novella when, following a dramatic encounter with Smolyanov, Grisha decides to change his life. At first, he is not sure what has to be done, but simply acknowledges "that something inside him had changed irrevocably... and he had become an altogether different person, with a different blood type and a different chemical makeup" (p. 346). When Grisha finally makes the crucial decision to leave Lyalya and to start a new life outside Moscow, he experiences a fantastic sensation of lightness, described by him as "something delightful and absurd. If he hadn't been afraid of making a fool of himself, he would have taken off from the ground and winged his way above the buildings" (p. 347).

In addition to the voices of Grisha and Lyalya, *The Long Goodbye* introduces the voices of two more characters, the playwright Smolyanov, and Lyalya's father Pyotr Telepnev. They are given relatively little space, but, nevertheless, succeed in bringing new dimensions to the story and illuminating the existing conflicts from different angles.

From the point of view of plot structure, the figure of Smolyanov is of prime importance: he is the third party in the love triangle involving Lyalya, Grisha and himself. He acts as a catalyst between the two protagonists, forcing them to reevaluate their relationship and to make final decisions. He is also an antipode to Grisha, showing how a mediocre playwright can forge a brilliant career, thanks to the support of an influential party official. Although his plays are described as "sycophantic" and "absolute rubbish," they are staged all over the country, including the prestigious Moscow Drama Theater.

The reader first sees Smolyanov through the eyes of Lyalya and Grisha, who depict him respectively as an unhappy and weak man, trying his best in the theater, and as an arrogant and ruthless one, taking advantage of others to promote his own career. Such a disparity of opinions reflects two totally different perspectives: that of a mistress, and that of a rival.

As it turns out, Grisha comes closer to understanding the essence of Smolyanov's character, revealed in the second part of the novella in the form of Smolyanov's indirect interior monologue. While reflecting on his difficulties in both his personal and professional life, Smolyanov displays a striking degree of egotism, complacency, and a total lack of consideration for others. He proves to be cynical and ruthless, ready to crush anyone standing in the way of his success.

Whereas Smolyanov plays an important role in the main story line, Lyalya's father Pyotr Telepnev develops a secondary theme, that of the inevitable changes brought by rapid urbanization and modernization. Faced with the prospect of losing his garden, which he had cultivated for three decades, Telepnev puts up a fierce fight, writing petitions to the housing administration and to the city's chief architect, requesting that his garden be preserved. Despite constant rejections, he keeps re-appealing, gathering the support of influential people and devising new arguments for his case. As could be expected, Telepnev's fight ends in failure: his garden has to yield to the construction of a new residential district, and he suffers two heart attacks and loses the will to live and fight for his case.

The theme of the helplessness of an individual against so-called "progress," introduced in Telepnev's narrative, widens the scope of the novella, moving it from the narrow frame of personal problems toward general questions of social and moral responsibilities. Only with this broad perspective can the reader grasp the true character of the novella's protagonists and understand the dramatic changes in their lives in the next two decades. Those changes are clearly indicated in the epilogue of the novella, where Lyalya is a resigned middle-aged woman, preoccupied with her family and the difficulties of her job at the Culture Club. She has lost her job as an actress, and now seems totally disinterested in the theater. Smolyanov's "lucky star" has also faded; he is finished as a playwright and subsists on income from renting his dacha. Only Grisha has forged a successful career as a screenplay writer, but even he is not altogether happy, frequently recalling the earlier years and reflecting "that those years when he was poor and discouraged, when he envied, hated, suffered, and lived almost like a beggar were actually the best years of his life. . ." (p. 352).

Another Life

Of all the Moscow novellas, *Another Life* is the most consistent in its use of the concealed narrator, rendering exclusively the point of view of Olga, a forty-year-old widow who tries to readjust to life after the sudden death of her husband Sergei Troitsky. Acting as the central intelligence, Olga registers and evaluates everything that happens in the story, but concentrates on depicting her life with Sergei and her feelings about him during his lifetime and after his death. As a result, the novella has two distinctive protagonists and two closely interwoven story lines.

The narrative of *Another Life* unfolds on two temporal planes, past and present; the latter is clearly subdued, offering just a few details of Olga's life and her feelings several months after Sergei's death. The core of the story takes place in the past in the form of Olga's recollections of her childhood, her youth and above all, her seventeen-year marriage to Sergei. The past also includes events after Sergei's death which illuminate Olga's relations with her daughter Irinka and her own mother-in-law, Alexandra Prokofevna.

Olga's ventures into the past are motivated realistically in the novella. Frequently her memory is set in motion by the sight of familiar objects that belonged to Sergei: his numerous folders, notebooks and notepads remind her of his long, but useless work on his dissertation, his difficulties with his supervisors, and the ultimate rejection of his thesis. Sergei's picture, on the other hand, brings back memories of happy moments in their life, such as their first summer in the Crimea, their wedding, or their trips to the dacha in Vasilkovo.

Occasionally, a meeting with a common acquaintance makes Olga recall the past; after seeing Louiza, she remembers Sergei's friendship with Louiza's husband Fedya, and their work at the Institute. That memory in turn leads to other memories, connected with Sergei's work in the Institute and his relations with Klimuk and others. Sometimes, a familiar place stirs Olga's memory; at the subway station, for example, she recalls a party a year earlier.

Most frequently, however, Olga's reminiscences about the past take place during sleepless nights, when she attempts to understand the reasons for Sergei's premature death. Every night she wakes up "as though someone had roused her with a familiar, malicious nudge: "think, think, try and understand!"[93] In spite of her efforts, Olga cannot find the answer, mainly because she tries to pass the guilt on to others, persistently denying her own culpability.

First of all, she blames Sergei himself, pointing to "his lack of the necessary coolness and stamina" and "the constant restlessness that was his undoing." She sees the core of his problems in his unwillingness to change:

> Year after year of disappointments gradually wore him down, drained his strength; he began to stoop and to weaken; yet some central core remained untouched, like a thin steel rod that bent but did not break. And that was the root of the trouble: he refused to change his innermost nature. This meant that, although he suffered agonies as a result of his many failures, lost faith in himself, frittered away his energies in enthusiasms so absurd they made people think he had taken leave of his senses, although he strained his poor heart with the fury of his despair and self-reproach, he still refused to break that invisible, steely core within himself. (pp. 62-63)

Secondly, she accuses Sergei's co-workers in the Historical Institute, who by their own intrigues ruined his chances for defending his dissertation and forced him to resign from the institute. Olga is particularly disappointed in Gena Klimuk, Sergei's university friend who used him to promote his own career.

The third person Olga blames is Darya Mamedovna, a leading Soviet parapsychologist who introduced Sergei to parapsychology, and, at least in Olga's mind, had an illicit affair with him. Although Olga's suspicions are never confirmed in the story, she remains convinced that Darya Mamedovna "was leading him astray, wanting to gain power over him" (p. 162).

In presenting the story of Sergei and herself, Olga relies almost exclusively on indirect interior monologue which transmits her thoughts and feelings in the third person singular. This narrative method gives the novella a false sense of detachment and objectivity, while in reality it is biased and one-sided.[94] Olga's bias is most evident in her depiction of Sergei. She constantly stresses his negative traits, such as "the vacillating and unmanly streak in his character" (p. 27), "his clumsiness and shyness in practical matters and personal relations" (p. 77), and "his lack of dedication and of will power" (p. 108). Unable to penetrate Sergei's thoughts, she carefully gives a detailed account of his facial expressions, his gestures and the tone of his voice. Only occasionally does Olga report Sergei's speech, and these short remarks reveal a great deal of truth about his feelings regarding his marriage and his relations at work. Early in the novella, she recalls that "he had said one night that if it weren't for Irinka he would leave Olga" (p. 17), and later she reports his demand "that she stop tormenting him" (p. 162). Both remarks clearly reveal Sergei's dissatisfaction with Olga and contradict the idealized picture of the marriage which she tries to convey.

In the same way, Sergei's brief comments on his work in the institute disclose his rejection of the intrigues and politics there, the dishonesty and self-seeking. When Gena tries to persuade Sergei to give some of his research material to his supervisor, he firmly refuses and calls him "a shit," and later comments to Olga "Finita la commedia" (p. 119).

Olga's own depiction of Sergei's work and research is in general sparse and superficial. Not familiar with his exact views on history and the individual, she frequently resorts to cliches or simplifications, describing his work as "grave robbery":

> From remarks that he made at various times she managed to piece together his guiding principle, which was that the individual is the thread stretching through time, the supersensitive nerve of history that can be teased out and separated—and from which one can then learn a great deal. Man, he used to say, is never reconciled with death, because implanted in him is a sense that the thread of which he forms a part is endless. It is not God who rewards man with immortality, nor is the concept of immortality instilled into him by religion, but by that innate, genetically coded awareness of being a link in an infinite chain. (p. 111)

Olga's lack of understanding extends to Sergei's fascination with parapsychology, but in this case she is even more critical and disapproving. She acknowledges that for Sergei it was "a form of escapism and an evasion of the failures that plagued him constantly," but at the same time she tries to open his eyes to its irrelevance and intellectual poverty. Throughout the narrative, she refers to parapsychology in derogatory terms, such as "trash," "junk," "nonsense," "garbage," and "unbelievable drivel" (pp. 162-63).

Even when she is talking strictly about Sergei, Olga reveals a great deal about herself. She contrasts his weak and indecisive character with her own strength and determination, his love of buffoonery and teasing with her seriousness, and his lack of assertiveness with her self-assurance and conceit. She prides herself on being totally rational and counterattacks Sergei's theory of the individual as a thread stretching through time with the belief that "everything began and ended with chemistry, in all the universe and beyond its bounds, there was nothing that could not be expressed in chemical formulae" (p. 111). Yet, at the same time she acknowledges her trust in instincts and in "the voice of prescience." She speaks of "some instinct" that prompted her to forbid Sergei from going on the trip on which his friend Fedya was killed, and of her "evil premonitions" about Darya Mamedovna.

There is a similar contradiction in Olga's attitude toward Sergei himself; on the one hand, she insists on her sincere love for him, while, on the other, she continues to torment him with her jealousy and her constant lectures. Her jealousy extends to women Sergei knew before her, as well as to the many potential rivals after their marriage, most notably their neighbor Zoika, Darya Mamedovna, and even wives of their common friends.

Olga's jealousy is matched by her strong desire to dominate Sergei. She created this role at the very beginning of their relationship and convinced herself that Sergei approved of it:

> Yet he seemed to enjoy being held by the hand, to enjoy her indignation on his account. It was perhaps at that moment that her mind created the model which for years she was to keep before her as the ideal form of their relationship, toward which she would strive with her utmost strength, and to which he cunningly pretended to submit, while remaining in fact remote and uninvolved: to lead him by the hand and teach him what was right, no matter what the cost in pain and heartache. (p. 29)

In recollecting her life with Sergei, Olga carefully conveys her feelings, stressing her anxieties and worries about Sergei's failures at work, his fascination with parapsychology, and his gradual drifting away from her. After his retreat to Vasilkovo, she speaks of "the nagging unease, the awareness of missing him, worrying about him," which gradually intensifies to "a sort of merciless, corrosive anxiety that grew inexorably within her" (p. 129). Olga's torments become even more pronounced when Sergei gets seriously involved in parapsychology: "she suffered torments," "was alarmed," "felt extremely hurt," "reduced to despair," (pp. 175-78), and so on.

Although at the beginning of the narrative Olga refuses to see her own guilt, she gradually begins to recognize her mistakes and expresses regret over her attitude toward Sergei. Recollecting their quarrel after Sergei's dissertation proposal was rejected, Olga remarks:

> . . . of course, she shouldn't have let her irritation show. . . She had to bite her tongue until it hurt, in order to prevent herself from shouting it out; because he really was in trouble and you don't hit a man when he is down." (p. 116)

She also expresses her regret over her inability to accept Sergei's views on the relations between history and the individual, his belief in the unbroken thread running from generation to generation. Referring to his philosophy, she first poses a rhetorical question: "Did he expect her, a biologist and a materialist, to put forward a refutation of these theories?" but then she reproaches herself: "If only she could refashion her cast of mind, even if only for a moment, but unfortunately it was not within her power" (p. 111). Having firmly opposed Sergei's idea of immortality with her simplistic theory that "everything begins and ends with chemistry," after his death she begins to question it herself: "My God, if everything begins and ends with chemistry, why was there such pain?"

The above passage is one of several instances where direct interior monologue is used to render Olga's thoughts on the meaning and purpose of life. As is typical of direct interior monologue, these passages abound in rhetorical questions, emphatic statements and exclamations. Responding to Sergei's idea of "another life":

> Olga felt her heart contract with fear. Where, for God's sake, was a new life to be found? What could possibly bring it about? Moving from one house to another? Buying a new briefcase? Going to this office instead of to that one? Basically, things were the same everywhere. (p. 181)

Olga's initial response to Sergei's need to change and start another life is that of bewilderment and unacceptance. She continues to question his idea in the months following his death. Eventually she learns to accept it, and to her own dismay, starts "another life" herself. This happens in the epilogue, which takes place several years after Sergei's death and portrays Olga sharing her innermost thoughts and love with another man. Her possessiveness and desire to dominate have given way to understanding and compassion now, her egotism—to love and concern.

Such an ending to the novella suggests that Sergei was correct in desiring that people learn "to get inside another person, to surrender oneself to another, to heal oneself through understanding" (pp. 180-81). Olga succeeded in moving away from the narrow realm of selfishness and self-absorption, and, as a result, attains "another life" which she poetically describes as being "as inexhaustible as that cold, windy expanse, vast as that boundless city fading from sight with the coming of evening" (p. 186).

The publication of the Moscow novellas aroused a heated polemic among Soviet critics and readers concerning Trifonov's method of representing reality, his portrayal of characters and his attitude toward the phenomena he describes. A large number of Soviet critics responded to the novellas negatively, denouncing Trifonov's preoccupation with *byt,* i.e., the details of everyday existence, and the lack of correlation between the "small" world of his characters and the "big" world of Soviet reality. In writing about *The Exchange, Taking Stock* and *The Long Goodbye,* G. Brovman reproached Trifonov for "showing the small, pitiful world of civic uselessness and moral dependence, without relying on the big world of Soviet reality":

> A writer can, of course, as Trifonov has done, put any phe-
> nomenon of life under his magnifying glass. But he ought not to
> ignore the multiform relations between that phenomenon and the
> advanced, progressive tendencies of actual reality. By ignoring these
> relations, these forces, that counterbalance that phenomenon, an
> artist unwillingly destroys... the normal, vital forces of society in his
> picture, and takes the risk of making incorrect social diagnoses and
> not defining future prospects correctly.[95]

A similar opinion was expressed by L. Fink, who, in his review of *Another Life,* described the novella as "giving a vivid and faithful depiction of everyday details, but failing to portray broader life":

> The action [of the novella], which is limited to family relations, is
> completely enclosed within the boundaries of the apartment. The
> contours of larger, real life are almost indiscernible, the lives of the
> heroes rarely cross with the paths of history. Trifonov therefore fails
> to give a broad, social interpretation of depicted phenomena....[96]

Critics and readers alike discussed at length the questions of the negative depiction of reality and the lack of positive models. V. Bednenko and O. Krinitsky, two engineers from the Kiev Polytechnical Institute, wrote to *Molodaya gvardiya,* sharply criticizing Trifonov for his portrayal of weak, uninspiring characters with petty interests and for "the butterfly existence" of the people surrounding them. After comparing *Taking Stock* with *The Exchange,* they concluded that the illness portrayed in the latter "has spread considerably, infecting more characters, and is threatening to become an epidemic." They reminded Trifonov that "...a writer should not restrict himself to the passive depiction of an illness...." He should support the tendency to renew life and literature, to create new heroes who could show others how to understand and eliminate the causes of that illness.[97]

The protagonists of *The Long Goodbye* and *Another Life* were given similar criticism. M. Gus characterized Rebrov as "an outsider, unable to understand the surrounding reality, or to become part of it," and all those around him as "typical representatives of the narrow-minded bourgeois class, living that impersonal life which existentialism considers the norm of everyday existence."[98] The writer V. Dudintsev rejected both protagonists of *Another Life* as "failures": Sergei for "his total lack of creative consistency and responsibility," and Olga for "her negative attitude towards everyone around her, and especially those who are successful."[99]

In an extension of the criticism of Trifonov's characters, many Soviet scholars charged that the writer had avoided clear and straightforward judgments, that he "hid behind the backs of his protagonists."[100] L. Andreev criticized the intangibility of Trifonov's characters, calling them "washed out and out of focus," a result, the critic claimed, of the author's "not knowing how to treat his characters."[101] Similar opinions were expressed by L. Anninsky, L. Fink, and I. Sozonova, who spoke respectively of "the author's uncertainty,"[102] "a lack of a definite position in the narrative structure," and "contradictions in the author's attitude towards his heroes."[103]

Responding to these accusations of uncertainty, some Soviet critics correctly pointed out that although Trifonov did not make any accusatory comments about his characters, the artistic logic of their behavior served as an indisputable exposure.[104] Grinberg, Amusin and Bazhenov saw Trifonov's characterization as a sign of his maturity rather than a shortcoming. Bazhenov wrote:

> Yury Trifonov is a complex writer; his prose is saturated with ideas and always demands maturity on the part of the reader in order that he participate creatively in the author's intentions.[105]

M. Amusin praised Trifonov for his perfect knowledge of his characters' psychology and his skill in dissolving his own identity in their internal world. Amusin cited Trifonov's ability to portray the interdependence and interrelationship between the small world of a private life and the large world of history, between the general and the intimate facts of an individual life, which arises from a combination of unique personal characteristics and is also determined by the spirit of the times.[106]

Amusin's views were supported by the critics V. Pertsovsky and N. Tyulpinov. In an article with the characteristic title, "Testing through *Byt*," Pertsovsky argued that *byt* is a most difficult test for man:

> Trifonov's heroes escape into everyday life to avoid the difficulties and problems of the larger world . . . but in this modest everyday life they encounter the same problems, even more complex and

intricate. Everyday existence in Trifonov's novellas becomes a dramatic moving force.[107]

In his review of *Another Life* N. Tyulpinov used the same argument in defense of *byt:*

> Trifonov's current fiction is very distinctive. It seems to dwell on the details of *byt*, but behind these details we can at first guess and then clearly see something else—the reality of emotional experiences which find expression in the ordinary circumstances of life.
> *Byt* is...the which characters prove themselves.[108]

Tyulpinov also acknowledged Trifonov's great skill in depicting the psychology of his characters, a quality praised by such prominent Soviet critics as A. Bocharov and F. Kuznetsov. Bocharov drew an interesting comparison between Trifonov's method of writing and the technique used to X-ray reality; he argued that the writer is concerned not so much with the details of everyday life as with the emotions and experiences of men in everyday situations.[109] Bocharov gave credibility to Trifonov's method of writing by acknowledging that he continued the tradition of Chekhov in conveying the dramatic essence of everyday life and disclosing the complexities and importance of man's surroundings.[110]

Some critics also drew a comparison between Trifonov and Dostoevsky, pointing out both writers' emphasis on ethical conflicts as well as their extraordinary skill in portraying their characters' social and psychological development.[111]

As a Soviet writer, Trifonov is generally placed together with Daniil Granin (1918-), Vladimir Tendryakov (1923-84), and I. Grekova (1907). With the exception of the last, these are of the same generation; they were born after the Revolution and raised during the tragic thirties, they lived through the Second World War, and made their literary debuts in the early fifties. Like Trifonov, these three writers tried out different genres but succeeded above all in reviving the novella. What makes their novellas similar is, first, their depiction of city life, for which critics have classified them as "urban" writers, and secondly and more importantly, their increased interest in the moral problems facing the contemporary Soviet intelligentsia. They differ, however, in the extent to which they pose moral questions and in their artistic treatment of these topics.

Tendryakov's works tend to rely on dramatic conflicts, which include murder, patricide or child abandonment. He deals with such sensitive problems quite openly, and seldom leaves any doubt as to his own position and his evaluation of events.[112] By contrast, the novellas of Granin and Grekova seem at first glance devoid of moral commentaries, simply portraying details of everyday existence and the heroes' daily routine.[113] But beyond the facade of normal life the reader meets questions of moral conduct, of compromising one's conscience, of conformity or dishonesty. What differentiates these two writers is their approach to narrative structure. Whereas Granin tends to use an omniscient narrator, Grekova prefers a personalized narrator who reproduces the protagonists' viewpoints. She relies heavily on interior monologue that reveals her characters' thoughts and feelings and on dialogues that strengthen their characterization.

Of the three writers discussed above, Grekova seems closest to Trifonov.[114] They share a deep interest in the life of the Soviet intelligentsia and in the psychology of contemporary city dwellers. Grekova, however, concentrates on the depiction of strong female characters who are successful at work, but who experience problems in their personal lives, whereas Trifonov presents a group portrait of "superfluous" male characters who find themselves dissatisfied with their work, their families, and even themselves. His heroes are examined more closely in relation to both their immediate families and their professional and social milieu than are Grekova's. And, Trifonov is more successful in conveying the complex inner worlds of his heroes, with their most intimate thoughts and feelings, their evaluation of everything and everyone around them. Characteristically, both writers prefer to trace moral problems without suggesting their resolution and without offering their own personal judgment. The reader must evaluate events and draw his own conclusions.

CHAPTER VII

THE HOUSE ON THE EMBANKMENT

Published in 1976, *The House on the Embankment* continues thematically, as well as artistically, the model which Trifonov established in his Moscow novellas. It depicts the ethics of human relations by probing the inner world of its characters and conveying this world through a concealed narrator who reproduces the protagonists' thoughts and emotions. *The House on the Embankment* widens the scope of the Moscow novellas, however, by more thoroughly examining the lives of several characters and presenting a picture of an entire generation. As a result, this work approaches the genre of the novel, whose magnitude permits a greater variety of characters, an ampler development of milieu, and a more sustained exploration of character.[115]

The widening of thematic scope is evident in the short prologue which suggests the novella's theme—how a group of young boys were transformed over time into different people. The prologue also establishes a dual temporal perspective—past and present. Exact temporal boundaries are not firmly established here; reference is simply made to the swift passage of time and to the fact that those boys who did survive the war and other catastrophes changed drastically, as if by magic. The prologue is narrated by an unidentified first-person voice whose role in the plot remains a mystery at this point.[116]

In the second paragraph the action moves to a specific temporal frame—August 1972—and to a specific incident that sets the entire plot in motion—a chance meeting between Vadim Glebov and his old friend Lev Shulepnikov. As the action unfolds, Glebov not only becomes the chief protagonist but also its central narrative voice. His perception of present events and his recollections of the past constitute the core of the plot and serve as a catalyst for its development. Stirred by Lev's refusal to recognize him, Glebov spends a sleepless night reconstructing his relations with his old friend from school and the university, and striving to understand what made Lev turn his back on him. The core of the novella is presented in the form of Glebov's recollections of the past, covering a span of thirty-five years; special attention is given to his school years in the late thirties, his university years a decade later, and a handful of reminiscences from the fifties and sixties.

Glebov's reminiscences do not follow any strict chronological or logical order. They skip back and forth between different times and places, mingling important events with minor details, and juxtaposing clear memories with somewhat blurred or distorted facts. The lack of chronology is apparent in all of Glebov's reminiscences: he begins with his recollections of Lev at the university in the late forties, and only later reconstructs their school years of a decade earlier; he first mentions Sonya in connection with her premature death, and only later describes her in school and at the university.

Frequently, Glebov combines distant events linked by the same person or a similar experience. Thus, while remembering the crucial meeting with Druzyaev in November of 1948, he also recalls the dean's dramatic downfall two years later, as well as his stroke and death in 1953. Similarly, his recollections of Sonya bring back the memory of his affair with an older woman in evacuation, as well as his popularity with female students in his early years as a teacher.

In some of his reminiscences Glebov juxtaposes important events with trivial details; while reconstructing his complex relations with Lev, he suddenly remembers the first kiss he received from Dina; his memory of his betrayal of his friends in 1938 is linked with the image of Professor Ganchuk greedily eating a French pastry after being destroyed at a meeting in 1948.

In terms of clarity, Glebov's reminiscences vary, from the very lucid to the somewhat blurred and even distorted. As the narrative progresses, it becomes evident that Glebov subconsciously tries to suppress certain painful memories, believing that "whatever one didn't remember ceased to exist" (p. 337). Thus, he tries not to remember the harsh words uttered by Kuno Ivanovich after Glebov's denunciation of Professor Ganchuk, the distorted face of Yulia Mikhailovna after her dismissal, or the critical remarks by Professor Ganchuk several years after his reinstatement. Above all, Glebov tries to forget the second meeting in March 1949, when he spoke against Professor Ganchuk:

Maybe it wasn't quite like that, because he was trying to forget it. Whatever one didn't remember ceased to exist. None of it had ever happened. There never had been that second, crowded meeting in March, when there was no longer any point in reproaching onself; he had to go anyway, and even if he didn't speak himself, he was at least obliged to listen to the others. He did, it seems, say something at that meeting, something very brief and of very little significance. It had completely escaped his memory. So what? It no longer mattered. Ganchuk's fate had already been decided. (p. 337)

While recollecting his past, Glebov concentrates on his own feelings—his emotional responses to the people and events around him. He devotes a great deal of attention to his complex relations with Lev, based simultaneously on "servile devotion and spiteful envy" (p. 199). From the very beginning of their acquaintance, Glebov is torn between his admiration for Lev's self-confidence and his resentment at "the unfairness of things," which made all the good things in life simply fall into Lev's lap, while Glebov had always to struggle for everything (p. 200). Glebov's deeply rooted resentment stems from the obvious discrepancies in status and living standards between the Shulepnikovs and the Glebovs. Whereas Lev's stepfather is an influential secret police official and can provide his family with a comfortable living in the exclusive "house on the embankment," the Glebovs are simple working people who live in a crowded communal apartment and can barely afford the basic necessities. Aware of these apparent injustices, the twelve-year-old Glebov is overwhelmed by "a leaden, sickening resentment," which he compares to "a chronic disease, at times severe, at times imperceptible, at other times so intense as to be unbearable" (p. 200). Glebov still feels resentment and envy towards Lev ten years later, at the university. He openly admits "the familiar depression" and "the leaden feeling that was forever linked with Shulepa" (p. 232). Once again he feels like "a poor relation or an impecunious friend of this darling of the fates" (p. 232).

Despite his antipathy and envy, Glebov is strongly drawn to Lev and turns to him for help in critical moments, such as during the official campaign against Professor Ganchuk, when Glebov is forced to take a stand: either to renounce his supervisor and future father-in-law, or lose his scholarship and forfeit his chances to do graduate work. Faced with this difficult decision, Glebov is overwhelmed by fear, described as "utterly despicable, blind, formless, like a creature born in a cellar" (p. 298). It is the same feeling he had experienced ten years earlier, when Lev's stepfather asked him to name the boys who had attacked his son. At that time the fear manifested itself physiologically in the form of a gnawing pain in his stomach and a loud and very obvious rumbling; it prompted Glebov to betray his two friends. In similar fashion, Glebov betrays Professor Ganchuk, initially by not attending the critical meeting and, subsequently, by openly speaking against him. Thirty years later, he attests to the genuine fear which existed at the time: "there secretly hovered... a nasty little skeleton called fear. For that, if nothing else, was genuine, even though one realized it much later" (p. 302).

In his cowardly denunciation of Professor Ganchuk, Glebov betrays not only his professor, but also the professor's daughter, Sonya, to whom he is engaged. Throughout the novella Glebov returns to his feelings about Sonya. On the one hand, he seems to be genuinely attracted to her, he admires her remarkable character, her kindness and devotion, he feels miserable in her absence and experiences a passionate desire to be close to her. On the other hand, he speaks of "post-coital depression," and an aversion to her touch, her caresses, even her voice (p. 299). Unable to comprehend his own feelings, Glebov turns to Lev for help, only to hear him comment sarcastically: "feelings, shmeelings" (p. 311), and propose a thousand-to-one odds that Glebov will abandon her (p. 314). Lev's straightforward reaction reveals the true character of Glebov's relationship with Sonya: it is based not on genuine love, but on a selfish desire to promote his own career and to gain access to the Ganchuk riches. The same conclusions are drawn by Sonya's mother, who accuses Glebov of "having made use of everything: her house, her dacha, her books, her husband and her daughter" (p. 342).

The opinions expressed by Lev, Yulia Mikhailovna and others allow the reader to distance himself from Glebov's one-sided presentation and interpretation of events. As expected, Glebov acts as a highly biased narrator, presenting a subjective perception of the action and a very personal evaluation of all the characters. He is particularly biased in his self-evaluation, constantly stressing his better qualities and trying to justify his most callous acts. Thus, while acknowledging the betrayal of his two school friends, he attempts to justify his actions by convincing himself that "it was fair, because those who would be punished were bad" (p. 231). He also tries to diminish the consequences of his denunciation: "nor did anything very terrible happen to the Bear or Manyunya either. The Bear's parents changed jobs and left Moscow, taking their son with them, and Manyunya got such bad grades that he was expelled from school" (p. 231). Similarly, Glebov tries to justify his betrayal of Sonya and her father. He charges Professor Ganchuk with arrogance and conceit, qualities that had turned his colleagues and students against him. As for Sonya, Glebov convinces himself that he had never loved her but was simply attracted to her physically: "What had it been? True love that had matured slowly and naturally, or the physical infatuation of youth which had suddenly struck them like a disease? Probably the latter" (p. 270).

If Glebov had been the sole narrator of the novel, the reader would have been exposed to only one version of events and an idealized image of the protagonist. But Trifonov introduces a second narrative voice into the novella, that of Glebov's nameless school friend. Like Glebov, the unidentified narrator reminiscences about his past, especially his school years; he complements Glebov's account with a different point of view and a different interpretation of the events that took place.[117]

The voice of the nameless narrator is clearly distinguished from that of Glebov by the use of the first person and an open bias against Glebov. The narrator does not hide his contempt for Vadim "The French Loaf" and his ability to be a "nothing person":

> He seemed to fit in with everybody: he was like this and he was like that; he got on with this bunch and that bunch; he wasn't bad and he wasn't good; he wasn't very selfish and he wasn't very generous; he was not exactly an *octopus* and not quite a *crap-eater* either; he was no coward, yet not noticeably brave; he didn't seem sly or cunning, yet at the same time he was not a simpleton. (pp. 272-73)

To illustrate this "nothing personality" of Glebov's, the narrator recalls a number of events: Glebov's clever way of joining "The Secret Society for Testing the Will," which allowed him to leave the society at any time; his conspiratorial arrangements with the street gang to avoid confrontation; and the way in which he used Sonya to stop the daring test of walking on the balcony railing. The narrator also reveals a great deal about Glebov's personality by contrasting the latter's artificial friendship with Lev with his own relationship with Anton. While Glebov is drawn to Lev for his wealth and status, the narrator is captured by Anton's intellect, courage and self-discipline.

Much of the narrator's attention is devoted to his move from the house on the embankment in the fall of 1938. The narrator stresses his feelings of shame and humility, of total loss, and his apprehension about the future. Described in a very reserved manner, this episode acquires a new meaning when juxtaposed with Glebov's account of his betrayal and the "harmless" consequences for the Bear and Manyunya. What seemed like a simple change of jobs for the Bear's parents proves to be closer to actual deportation and the separation of parents and children; and Manyunya's expulsion from school leads him to the reformatory, and eventually to a prison camp.

The "moving out" episode allows the reader to establish the identity of the second narrator, who turns out to be Yura the Bear, one of the "bad" boys denounced by Glebov. The Bear is evidently unaware of Glebov's role in his parents' downfall; his antagonism is based solely on a feeling of rivalry for the affection of their schoolmate Sonya, who is blinded by her love for Glebov and fails to notice Yura altogether.

The core of the second narrator's story concerns the events of 1937-38, but he also offers a brief account of the early war years and the subsequent fates of his school friends. That account fills in the gap in Glebov's story, providing information on the real tests of willpower which took place during the war and the ways the boys responded to them. Some, like Glebov, chose the easy way out, joining the evacuation; others, like Anton and Walrus, volunteered for the front and never returned. Following his brief account of the war experiences, the narrator disappears from the novella, only to reappear briefly in the epilogue, which is set in 1974.[118] Here he informs the reader about his work on a book about the 1920s, his meeting with old Professor Ganchuk, and their visit to Sonya's grave at Donskoi Cemetery. At the cemetery they become involved in an argument with the groundskeeper, who turns out to be none other than Lev Shulepnikov.

This chance encounter between the second narrator and Lev provides a parallel for the meeting between Glebov and Lev that took place at the beginning of the novella. Thus the entire work is given a frame-like composition. Both meetings have a shocking effect on the respective narrators, since they show "that darling of the fates" transformed into a wretched old man, drinking to excess and working at the lowest jobs. Not unexpectedly, Lev chooses not to recognize his former schoolmates. Without doubt, he experiences shame and humiliation, but, at least in the case of Glebov, he also feels contempt. When Lev telephones Glebov late at night, he confesses:

> "I really used to dislike you. . . . Hey, did you hear that, Vadim, for Christ's sake? I mean what I say: I really disliked you."
>
> "But why?" asked Glebov, yawning.
>
> "God knows. You never did me any harm, really. I guess you must be a doctor or a professor or some kind of big wheel now, the cherry on top of a cake of shit. I couldn't care less, though. Doesn't bother me. I'm not in that ball game." (p. 195)

A scoundrel himself, Lev despises Glebov for his lack of moral principles and his ruthless pursuit of his own interests. He is not impressed with Glebov's position as a professor, because he knows what price had to be paid to achieve it.

Characteristically, Lev does not respond to the second narrator either, perhaps wrongly identifying him with the establishment. But the meeting with this narrator has a positive influence on Lev: as he rides home he looks up at the house on the embankment and wonders "whether some miracle might happen and another change might take place in his life" (p. 350).

The meeting with the second narrator brings back happy memories of childhood, when the young boys strived to achieve virtue and self-discipline. Some of them, like Anton and Walrus, had only one chance to prove themselves in real life: they volunteered for the war and were killed defending their country. Others, like the narrator, returned from the war and lived according to the high ethical principles of their youth. Still others, most notably Glebov and Shulepnikov, strayed from their path of moral integrity by exploiting everyone and everything for their own advancement. Ironically Shulepnikov, who had the clear advantage of a privileged position, never achieved any success, while the insipid Glebov made a brilliant career by using the "right connections" and stepping over anyone standing in his way.

In view of the above, it becomes clear that the introduction of the second narrator widens the scope of the novel, moving it from the theme of the moral disintegration of one individual to the broader picture of an entire generation, born after the revolution and shaped during the late thirties and forties. It is true that the historical background of the tragic decade of Stalinist terror and the painful experiences of World War II is drawn sparsely, but the novel does succeed in showing the link between the character of an individual and his environment. Although no direct judgments are made in the work, the reader has no problem seeing Glebov as the product of the Stalinist era, when fear and concern for self-preservation ruled the lives of the Soviet people. Similarly, the reader can see Lev Shulepnikov as a typical child of the establishment, cynically taking advantage of his privileged position during Stalin's lifetime, but losing everything in the post-Stalinist period. By contrast, the son of the family unjustly repressed in the purges proves to be an honest man, living his life according to ethical principles. Despite his moral integrity, however, he is not to be regarded as a "positive hero," for, as Soviet critics pointed out, he is too passive and lacks the qualities of a born leader.[119]

Inasmuch as the historical events of the thirties and early forties are relegated to the background of the novel, the political reality of the late forties, especially the campaign against so-called cosmopolitanism and formalism, stands at the center of Glebov's narrative.[120] The case against Professor Ganchuk constitutes the central conflict to advance the plot and reveals the true nature of Glebov's personality.

It is interesting to note the remarkable parallel between *The House on the Embankment* and *Students*, written some twenty-five years earlier. Both novels portray the purges that took place at Soviet universities between the years 1948 and 1951, but while *Students* oversimplifies the conflict and concentrates on an idealized student collective, the later work puts the purges at the center of the plot, and focuses on the personal involvement of the protagonists. Unlike Vadim Belov, who believed in the guilt of Professor Kozelsky, Glebov is very much aware of the unfairness of the accusations made against Professor Ganchuk. Yet he lets himself be used to promote his own academic career. Moreover, while *Students* provides a happy resolution to the conflict, by allowing Professor Kozelsky to admit his mistakes and be reinstated at the university, *The House on the Embankment* shows the tragic consequences for both Professor Ganchuk and his family: after his dismissal he suffers a stroke, and when he is reinstated, he returns a sick old man; his wife loses her job and soon dies; their daughter Sonya has a nervous breakdown and is confined to a psychiatric asylum. Although Glebov refuses to admit his involvement, he is responsible for the destruction of the Ganchuk family. Through their pain and despair, he was able to advance his career and now enjoys the comfortable life of a university professor.

The similarities between these two novels prompted some critics to consider *The House on the Embankment* a "revised" version of *Students*.[121] Indeed, it seems that after a twenty-five-year delay Trifonov responded to the critics' suggestion, and rewrote his novel, giving it a new focus and a new interpretation. In place of an idealized student collective and a positive hero, he presented the chilling picture of cowardliness and opportunism which prevailed at Soviet universities in the post war-years and encouraged some faculty members and students to abandon their moral principles in favor of personal advancement.

The emphasis on moral and psychological problems brings *The House on the Embankment* close to many novels about science and scientists written in the 1970s, including: V. Bondarenko's *Pyramid*, A. Kron's *Insomnia*, V. Kaverin's *Two-hour Stroll*, I. Grekova's *Faculty*, and many others.[122] Unlike the novels of the 1960s, which tended to explore the relationship between science and politics or science and ideology, the works of the 1970s depict the intellectual and psychological problems of individual scientists confronted with internal bureaucracy and corruption, dishonesty, and careerism. The range of disciplines depicted in the novels also expanded—from the exact sciences like physics or cybernetics, to social sciences and humanities.[123]

While following the same general tendency, i.e. depicting the political and ideological struggles in the humanities and concentrating on individual characters' moral dilemmas, Trifonov proved to be most consistent in treating this subject psychologically, from the point of view of the character who makes compromises with his conscience. With his unique focus on the psychology of a "negative" character, Trifonov succeeded in *The House on the Embankment* in presenting an anatomy of betrayal which begins as a small compromise, but leads eventually and inexorably to a total disregard for ethical norms.

CHAPTER VIII

IMPATIENCE

&

THE HISTORICAL NOVEL

Simultaneously with his work on the Moscow novellas, Trifonov wrote *Impatience*, a historical novel dealing with the activities of the nineteenth-century Russian revolutionary group The People's Will. The novel was written for the series "Ardent Revolutionaries" and was initially published in *Novy Mir*, then later by the Political Science Press in 1973.[124] The switch from the contemporary themes of the Moscow trilogy to the historical past did not prevent Trifonov from closely analyzing his heroes and their motivation for joining the terrorist group. The novel focuses on the figure of Andrei Zhelyabov, who, as a populist, hoped to bring about changes in Russia by educating the peasants, but who eventually accepted terror as the best means of achieving that end. The novel traces Zhelyabov's transformation, showing the reasons why "this son of a peasant, a student, a peaceful man, a fan of Lermontov and Taras Bulba" gradually accepted killing.

Trifonov's preoccupation with the psychological aspect of terrorist activities sets *Impatience* apart from numerous novels about The People's Will written in the seventies.[125] The majority of those depict the history of that group in documentary-like fashion, such as M. Popovsky's *Conquered Time* and V. Voinovich's *The Extent of Trust*. A dependence on factual material also marks I. Davydov's trilogy, *March, In the Desolate Autumn*, and *My Bequest to You, Brothers*, although all three novels include some psychological analysis. The only work that matches *Impatience* in terms of its psychological approach to the question of terror is V. Dolgy's *The Threshold*, which portrays the life of Sofia

Perovskaya, who renounced her aristocratic background to join the revolutionaries.[126] All the above novels depict the history of The People's Will through the activities of its individual members, as a rule, those in charge of the organization. For example, *The Threshhold* tells the unusual story of Sofia Perovskaya, while *The Extent of Trust* depicts the somewhat similar fate of Vera Finger. Davydov's novels focus on the lives of German Lopatin and Alexander Mikhailov, while Popovsky's *Conquered Time* portrays the biography of Nikolai Morozov.

Similarly, *Impatience* places the story of Andrei Zhelyabov at the center of its narrative. The novel focuses on the last three years of his life, beginning in 1878 when he leaves his wife and son to devote himself totally to the revolution, and ending with his execution in 1881. Including flashbacks, however, the time span covers more than twenty years: the book offers a picture of Andrei's childhood in the village, his student years at the university, his work as a tutor in Gorodishche, his marriage to Olga Yakhnenko and their life in Odessa. All these recollections stress the oppressive nature of the tsarist system against which Zhelyabov rebelled: the abduction of his aunt Lyuba as the landlord's mistress, which he witnessed as a child; the mistreatment of a Jewish student, which led to a student rebellion and Zhelyabov's expulsion from the university; and finally his arrest and imprisonment for participating in the populist movement. Acquitted in 1877, Zhelyabov, nevertheless, returned from prison a convinced revolutionary determined to dedicate his life to overthrowing the tsarist regime. For that reason he left his family, moved to St. Petersburg and began his life as an underground revolutionary.

The largest part of *Impatience* describes Zhelyabov's participation in the formation of The People's Will and its terrorist activities, in both of which he acted as one of the leaders. The reader learns about the congresses in Lipetsk and Voronezh, where the radical section split from the group and established a terrorist platform. Numerous attempts on the life of the Tsar followed—an unsuccessful bombing of his train and the Winter Palace, and, finally, his assassination on March 1, 1881. The novel ends with a detailed description of the trial that followed and the execution of the six terrorists, including Zhelyabov, who was arrested on the eve of the assassination but insisted on being included in the trial. He wrote to the new Tsar:

> If the new Tsar, having received his scepter from the hands of the Revolution, is determined to treat the Tsar's murderers by the rules of the old system; if Rysakov is to be executed, it would be a great injustice to spare my life [since] I attempted to assassinate the Tsar

several times and did not participate physically in the final assassination only as a result of ill luck. I insist on being included in the case and, if necessary, will provide testimony exposing my participation.[127]

Though central to the novel's structure, the story of Zhelyabov is part of a multi-layered plot, which presents the history of The People's Will and the role played by its leading members. The novel introduces a great number of characters involved in the group, with some appearing as secondary characters, while others receive a full-fledged characterization. Of the latter group, the most prominent are the figures of Alexander Mikhailov, the chief organizer of the group; Grishka Goldenberg, who assassinated Kropotkin, the governor of Kharkov and who then turned into an informer while under arrest; Stepan Khalturin, who single-handedly organized the bombing in the Winter Palace; Vanichka Okladsky, an expert in explosives, who for decades remained an agent for the police; and Nikolai Rysakov, one of the participants in the final assassination, who tried to save himself by betraying his comrades.

Impatience is particularly concerned with the anatomy of betrayal, studying the psychology of people like Goldenberg, Okladsky and Rysakov. The most interesting portrait is that of Goldenberg, who turned into a traitor not out of fear or weakness, but as a result of his vanity. Tricked by the prosecutor into believing that his cooperation with the authorities would help to restore peace and enact a constitution, he provided detailed information on his friends and their activities in an eight-page manuscript and a seventy-four page supplement. Characteristically, Grishka does not see himself as a traitor, but as a Messiah whose mission is to save Russia. Before his final break he has a recurrent dream in which he descends from the sky, like Christ, and addresses the government and the revolutionaries at a trial where all are being judged: Tsars, ministers, gendarmes, terrorists, and advocates of a peaceful platform. The trial ends with solemn choral singing, and all the participants have tears in their eyes.

Grishka is contrasted in the novel with Alexander Mikhailov, the chief organizer of The People's Will. Grishka's conceit and vainglory are juxtaposed with Mikhailov's depth and inner strength, his modesty and authority. Despite his young age (he is in his early twenties), he exercises a great deal of authority over his comrades, and is influential in organizing the split between the terrorists and the populists. Believing in a centralized and highly disciplined party, he takes on the project of writing a constitution and secures the support of his friends to adopt it. More than just a theoretician, he is the chief organizer of the group's terrorist actions; he masterminds the attempts to assassinate the Tsar, assigns tasks, and supervises the work of Kletochnikov, a double agent working for the police and The People's Will. Mikhailov appears in the novel as an example of a perfect revolutionary, renouncing his personal life in order to dedicate himself completely to the cause.

The story of Zhelyabov and The People's Will is set against the vast background of social and political life in post-reform Russia.[128] The novel presents the life of the peasantry, freed from serfdom, but still struggling to survive, like the family of Zhelyabov's maternal grandfather, Gavril Frolov. It depicts the hopes for reforms among the liberal intelligentsia, typified in the novel by Zhelyabov's father-in-law Yakhnenko and the well-known Russian writers Leo Tolstoy and Fyodor Dostoevsky. Even more vividly the novel presents the ruling class of Russia, from the tsarist bureaucracy and the police to Loris Melikov and the Tsar himself. Tsar Alexander II appears in the novel as a weak ruler, far more interested in his private life than politics. With his approval, the police and courts apply extremely harsh measures to crush the opposition; jails are overcrowded with terrorists, and a great number of them are sentenced to death or sent to Siberia. Loris Melikov, the head of the Supreme Administrative Commission who supervises the work on the new constitution, has some positive influence on the Tsar. Ironically, the Tsar approves the project on the day of his assassination, and it is cancelled by his successor.

In addition to a vast panorama of Russian society, the novel describes a wide range of locations. The action begins in Odessa and moves to rural areas in the Crimea and an estate in Southern Russia. In the Crimea the Tsar's summer residence and the port of Sevastopol are also shown. When Zhelyabov joins the revolutionaries, the action moves back and forth between Kiev, Lipetsk, Voronezh, Moscow, and St. Petersburg, the center of The People's Will activities. The novel offers a detailed topography of St. Petersburg, depicting the locations of the terrorists' presses, their meeting places and living quarters. In particular, the novel traces the routes taken by the Tsar, which were carefully studied by the terrorists while mapping their assassination spots.

The novel has a very complex narrative structure.[129] In addition to the objective voice of an omniscient narrator, it offers the subjective viewpoints of Zhelyabov and other major characters, as well as the voices of contemporaries, commenting on the events they have witnessed. Whereas "the voices" are clearly identified in the novel by the use of the first-person singular and the assignation of proper names, the transitions between the voices of the omniscient narrator and a concealed narrator, used to render the perspectives of individual characters, are not as clear. Both types of narration use the third-person singular, and rely on a sophisticated literary style.

Only a careful reading of the novel reveals the distinction between the general comments of an omniscient narrator and the subjective perception of events by individual characters. The omniscient narrator provides overall information on the situation in Russia, summarizes events not depicted in the novel, and is used to make transitions from a panoramic view to specific situations. The concealed narrator, on the other hand, reconstructs the points of view of individual protagonists through their perception of events and other characters. Predictably, the largest portion of the narrative reproduces the viewpoint of Zhelyabov, the undisputed protagonist of the novel. Those parts include not only his reminiscences, but also the story of the formation of The People's Will and its major activities. Through the eyes of Zhelyabov the reader learns about the meetings in Lipetsk and Voronezh, the assassination attempts in Aleksandrovsk and St. Petersburg, and, finally, the trial and the last minutes before the execution. The reader sees most of the revolutionaries through Zhelyabov's eyes, including Mikhailov and Tikhomirov, Okladsky and Goldenberg, Perovskaya and Finger. Most importantly, we learn from Zhelyabov himself about his state of mind and his feelings in regard to what was happening in Russia.

Zhelyabov's point of view is seldom reproduced directly as an interior monologue; more frequently it is given through indirect discourse: the hero's thoughts and observations are signalled by verbs of perception and thinking, suggestions of evaluation and reasoning. Here is the description of Zhelyabov's state of mind shortly before the execution:

> Shameful hearses turned out to be ordinary carts, only much higher. A bench for sitting was two *sazhens* from the ground. It looked absurd, like everything else: some gray pants, a black prisoner's coat, a black cap without a peak... All the time, whenever possible, Andrei looked at Sonia, and she looked at him. He had never seen this kind of a look on her face... A huge man with a spade-like beard came up to the cart. He had a grayish face, like a gray stone washed out by rain, but small, blue bear-like eyes sparkled in this gray. He immediately twisted Andrei's arms; at first there was an impulse to resist, but what for? He guessed that this man was the executioner... All of this ran through his mind, but he was dying to get beyond the gate, to see the streets, the crowd and the faces of the people, their looks and voices. His whole being was straining from this strong last desire. They put a board on his chest with a sign "regicide." His heart was beating. Faster! Faster! He will see and understand. No rewards, no farewells to this earth, just the eyes of the people. (pp. 651-52)

In a similar fashion, the novel reconstructs the points of view of other major characters, most notably those of Tsar Alexander II, the double agent Kletochnikov, the terrorists Grishka Goldenberg and Nikolai Rysakov. In all these cases, the emphasis is on the inner world of the characters, their strengths and weaknesses. This method of inner characterization helps to reveal the true nature of each personality; thus behind the external appearance of might and power, the reader learns about the Tsar's weak and indecisive character, while the seemingly downtrodden and frightened clerk Kletochnikov displays a surprising degree of courage and dedication.

A great deal of attention is devoted to the depiction of the inner struggle experienced by the two terrorists in the face of death. But while Grishka Goldenberg's voice is conveyed in the more subdued form of indirect discourse, Rysakov is given an opportunity to speak directly. Rysakov's voice is one of several "voices" directly reproducing the opinions of people involved in the movement and some of their contemporaries. Subjective as they are in their evaluation, these voices throw a new light on the events and history of The People's Will. Several of the voices comment in particular on Zhelyabov and the changes he went through in his short life, thus helping to establish a more objective picture of him.

The comments of Clio, the Muse of History, given almost a century later, perform a different function. They provide information on the fates of all the participants of the group and function as "micro-epilogues," concluding all the plot lines of the novel. Owing to these "micro-epilogues," the reader learns about the crushing of The People's Will and the tragic end of most of its members. But neither Clio nor the omniscient narrator gives a clear-cut evaluation of the group and its methods, leaving it to the reader to draw his own conclusions on the role of The People's Will in Russian history.

Stylistically, all the narrative lines are sustained in a restrained, sophisticated language, characteristic of well-educated, intelligent heroes. The novel primarily reproduces indirect speech, but there are instances of direct dialogue as well. The dialogues, however, lack any clear speech individualization, as if stressing the protagonists' common qualities.

The novel offers very few descriptions of nature, with the exception of the beginning, which presents Zhelyabov's recollections of childhood and his return to his village after his first imprisonment. The images of nature here are distinguished by calmness and serenity. There is a total indifference to human problems:

> Nothing had changed here: the same hot, green plain, turning yellow from the hot spring sun—it will become dry and brown in a

month—the same road, looping with misty humps into the pale, looming distance, the sky burning with the great heat, the sound of crickets, the cart moving far away. There was the beginning of his road, and he was saying good-bye to all of it. He knew he would never return here. And the world he was leaving behind was fresh, filled with sunshine, indifferent and invincible. (pp. 315-16)

By contrast, the later depictions of nature convey sordid qualities, such as gloominess, dirt and stench. Frequently, there is an underlying suggestion of death and graves, as in this description of the Aleksandrovsk ravine:

The bad autumn weather had come, cold and rainy. Streams of water were filling the huge ravine with dirt; they had to lie there motionlessly, like in a coffin, waiting. Like a cemetery, covered by flood waters, coffins were swimming in the cold water in black pre-winter darkness. (p. 418)

The associations with graves and darkness reappear in the description of tunnel digging in St. Petersburg:

They were working in the sap only at night. When they cut the drain, the sap was filled with a terrible stench. No one, not even Esaev, could stay there longer than three minutes, despite covering noses and mouths with respirators containing cotton moistened in chloride. (p. 592)

Along with the references to cemeteries and graves, there are frequent images of death, which serve to underline the tragic fates of all the heroes, who perish one by one, either on guillotines or in Siberia. Waiting for the explosion of the tsarist train, Andrei comes to the conclusion that:

... all life is waiting for death. But we do not notice. The waiting is deep inside us, in the depth of our beings, and when it comes up and penetrates and seizes us—the deadly waiting—then it is almost as if death itself had come. (p. 420)

The feeling of the inevitability of death permeates the entire novel; it is felt at times of risk as well as during happy moments. During a joyous and rowdy New Year's party, Andrei senses the presence of a deadly calmness:

A day earlier they had celebrated at Gesia Gelfman's apartment. Andrei did not remember such a happy commotion, stamping and dancing for a long time. Perhaps in his entire life there was nothing as lively... But behind all that noise, Andrei felt a deadly silence. He looked at the faces of his friends, suddenly realizing that he might be seeing them all together for the last time. (pp. 586-87)

The feeling of doom underlines the depiction of the love between Zhelyabov and Sonya Perovskaya. Their first encounter is described as follows:

And in this room there was love that had no past and no future, no hopes and no dawn. Cleansed from everything, it fell like snow, and like snow, it had to disappear. (p. 483)

Both Andrei and Sonya realize that their love will be short-lived and that their fates are predictable, but they accept this with a remarkable valour. Shortly before his arrest, Andrei tells Sonya: "...nothing will stop us. Even if we try to stop ourselves" (p. 600). And Sonya repeats these words just before the assassination: "There is no choice. Because no one can stop them anymore" (p. 622).

Although they think of events as inevitable, Andrei and Sonya and the other members of the group are anxious to precipitate events and lack the patience to wait for the achievement of their goals. The novel's title refers to the overwhelming sense of impatience which governs their actions and their thoughts. "History is moving too slowly," Zhelyabov reflects, "one has to urge it along." And Dvornik echoes: "Push history! Drive the old mare on! There is no time for long discussions. The issue of *The People's Will* has to come out on time: it is like an admiral's flag on a battleship, signalling readiness for battle" (p. 480).

Unlike the critical response to the Moscow novellas, the reviews of *Impatience* were unanimously positive. All the critics praised the novel's emphasis on the interaction of political and moral factors, and singled out the convincing psychological portrayal of the revolutionaries, "who could not accept social injustice and personal indignity, and responded to it with determination and self-sacrifice."[130] Most of the reviewers concentrated on the ideological and thematic aspects and overlooked the structural complexity of the novel.[131] One of the few exceptions was A. Filatova, who discussed Trifonov's skillful use of documentary material, the testimony of eye-witnesses and the perspective given by the posterior evaluation of historical events.[132] A similar positive evaluation of the novel's complex structure was given by M. Perelygina, who showed how "the voices" and Clio-72 introduced new dimensions and concluded all the plot lines.[133]

Trifonov himself emphasized the connection between his historical novel and the contemporary Moscow novellas, stressing that in all of them he attempted "to see, to show the fast flow of time, what it does to the people, how it changes everything... I want the reader to grasp the idea that the mysterious thread connecting different times goes through you and me, and that it constitutes the nerve of history."[134] In the same interview, "To Imagine Infinity," he also pointed out that the novel he was presently working on "partly borders on *Impatience*, and partly—on the Moscow novellas. Its action takes place at the time of the Civil War as well as today. Imagine a person who has lived to the present, but who has met people who remembered The People's Will, the explosion at the Ekaterinsky canal." The novel Trifonov cited was *The Old Man,* which indeed juxtaposed a historical theme with contemporary events, posing the question of how the times shape men's characters and fates.

CHAPTER IX

THE OLD MAN

The Old Man, written in 1978, continues to develop Trifonov's favorite theme of the influence of changing times and circumstances on an individual's formation, this time on the Old Guard Bolshevik Pavel Letunov.[135] Letunov fought in the Revolution and the Civil War, worked on industrial projects in the 1930s, was unjustly prosecuted in 1935, and following his rehabilitation in the mid-fifties, began interceding for the impeached Cossack commander Migulin.

In addition to the colorful past, which covers a span of sixty years, *The Old Man* portrays contemporary events in the mid-fifties in Sokolinyi Bor, a small resort near Moscow. The novel opens with a letter to the hero from his childhood love Asya. Her letter introduces a dual perspective: she tells Letunov about her present life and reminisces about the past. The letter is received in July 1974, and that date marks the beginning of the present events, which unfold in a sequence of several days in July and two days in August. The action then moves to November, again encompassing just a few days.

The present events concern the battle of several families over a small cottage vacated by the death of an old woman. Letunov, who at first does not want to have anything to do with the case, succumbs to the pressure of his family and decides to use his authority to win the cottage. The whole case proves futile, however, for at the end of the novel it is learned that the cottage, along with other buildings, will be demolished to make room for a new development.

The present events are transmitted in the novel essentially by three characters, all involved in the conflict over the cottage: Letunov, a seventy-three-year-old veteran of the Civil War and a respected member of the co-operative; Kandaurov, a forty-five-year-old employee of the Ministry of Foreign Affairs; and Izvarin, an enigmatic figure in the novel, who lived in Sokolinyi Bor as a child, but whose present affairs remain largely unknown to the reader. The role of each of these characters in the narrative varies. Letunov acts as the chief narrator, and the other two play episodic but, nevertheless, significant roles.

Of the three, the character of Izvarin is the least pronounced; he appears in only one episode in which the co-operative chairman Prikhodko unsuccessfully tries to lure him into the inheritance battle. Izvarin is totally disinterested in the offer, but the meeting with Prikhodko brings back memories of his childhood years in Sokolinyi Bor between the years 1926 and 1938, the origin of the co-op, and the interrelations of the five families who founded it. Izvarin's memories, which are transmitted indirectly in the third person, play an important role in elucidating the roots of the present conflict and throwing an additional light on the people involved in it.

In transmitting Kandaurov's point of view, the narrative deals not with the past, but with the present. Kandaurov, an unscrupulous man, is the only contender deeply involved in the case. He is determined to achieve his goal at any price, believing that "if you want to get something, you have to strain every nerve, use all the means and possibilities, everything, everything . . ." (p. 97). The reader comes to know Kandaurov rather intimately, owing to the uninhibited disclosures of his thoughts and his total frankness in revealing the real motives behind his actions. The indirect third-person narrative, conveying Kandaurov's point of view, frequently switches into a direct interior monologue.

Kandaurov is the direct opposite of Letunov, a man of total honesty and integrity. A typical idealist, Letunov is genuinely disinterested in material possessions, and for a long time resists the pressure of his family to get involved in the "cottage case." His lack of interest in the case is evident in his narrative, which conveys the details of everyday routine and the strained relations with his family, but avoids the controversy over the cottage.

As the central narrator in the novel, Letunov is present in four-fifths of the narrative, and his point of view clearly predominates. In those sections where Letunov narrates the present events, the third person is used almost exclusively, which gives the narrative a sense of detachment and objectivity. The usage of the more intimate first person occurs in the final episode of the novel: the meeting between Letunov and Asya, whom he has not seen for fifty-five years. The switch to the first person emphasizes the importance of the meeting and effectively conveys the hero's feelings. It also connects this episode with the past events, which are rendered exclusively in the first person: Letunov's recollections of his childhood, his love for Asya, his participation in the Civil War, and his fascination with Migulin, one of the Cossack commanders in the Don region. Unlike present events, which are told chronologically, the past unfolds as a series of seemingly disjointed episodes which make a coherent whole only at the novel's end.[136] The first event, which Letunov recalls after receiving Asya's letter, is the dramatic murder of nineteen Red Army men by the Filipov band in February 1919. His memory then leaps a year forward and pictures Asya in Rostov, sick with typhus, and worrying about her lover Migulin. Having recalled these two memorable events from the time of the Civil War, Letunov goes back in his reminiscences to the years 1915-17, and recalls the most important experiences of his boyhood and youth: his innocent love for Asya and his friendship with her cousin Volodya, the return from exile of his uncle Shura and Letunov's growing attachment to him, and the stormy events of 1917 and Letunov's involvement in the Bolshevik movement.

The events of 1917 are shown in the novel from the point of view of the adolescent Letunov, who cannot fully grasp the meaning of what is happening and simply reports the facts he is witnessing. Thus, Pavel speaks of the "drunken spring" of 1917 with thousands of people in the streets burning papers in front of the Police Headquarters, and red flags everywhere, even on the fortress and the Winter Palace. As the months go by, Pavel witnesses clashes between different political groups, the split in the Igumnov family, and the forced retreat of the Bolsheviks underground. Gradually, under the influence of his uncle Shura and the sailor Savva, Pavel gets personally involved in Bolshevik activities, selling *Pravda* and collecting money for the Workers' Council. When the October Revolution takes place, he welcomes it wholeheartedly and begins to work with Shura in the committee organizing the Red Army.

What seems in the eyes of the young Pavel like a straightforward path toward the revolution, however, looks far more complicated to the mature Letunov, who honestly admits that his involvement in the Bolshevik movement was not the result of the deliberate exercise of a strong will, but a matter of coincidence and fate: "I was a boy drunk with the powerful times. No, I don't want to lie like the others; the road was suggested by the stream, it is joyous to be in the stream" (p. 43). From the perspective of nearly sixty years Letunov acknowledges that he might have ended up on the opposite side, had he followed his father, his schoolteachers or Asya's family.

Having sketched the early stage of his life, Letunov returns to the period of the Civil War, which proved to be even more crucial for his development. Admitting his naiveté and lack of experience, he speaks of his difficulty in accepting the atrocities of the War and in understanding the intricate political maneuvering behind the scenes. He was fascinated with the figure of Migulin, both as a popular commander and as Asya's lover, and he could not comprehend the aura of mistrust and ill will surrounding the man. He also could not reconcile himself to the tough policies against the Cossack population recommended by Moscow and followed vigorously by some of his colleagues. Letunov's position was extremely difficult, for he sat on the Military Tribunal and was expected to act firmly and relentlessly.

As a member of that Tribunal, Letunov was one of those who sentenced Migulin to death for his unauthorized departure from the front in August 1919. Almost sixty years later, Letunov, still feeling the pangs of remorse, tries to understand what made Migulin undertake such a drastic step, and what his actual plans might have been. He recalls the major events that he witnessed in the Don region and looks at the archival materials that he had collected over the years which are kept in a special file entitled "Everything about Migulin."[137] These documents include fiery proclamations written by Migulin during the Civil War, his correspondence with headquarters, and the transcript of Migulin's trial in Bolshov in October 1919. These semi-authentic documents incorporated into the novel are intended to help the reader, as well as Letunov, find an answer to Migulin's complex character. They point to the impossibility of defining a person in single terms of "good" or "bad", "black" or "white." In Letunov's words:

> My God! How difficult it is to explain everything in one word. But they try it all the time. They tried when Migulin was alive, shouting the words "traitor" and "betrayer," and they are trying now with the shouts "a follower of Lenin," and "a revolutionary." If one could explain it simply by one word, I would not sit in the middle of the night, turning pages. (p. 148)

In recollecting the Civil War, Letunov does not restrict himself to Migulin, but introduces other Bolsheviks, most notably his uncle Shura, Shegontsev, Braslavsky, Orlik and others. Of these only Shura, a life-long professional revolutionary who had spent seven years in Siberia, seems to possess the qualities necessary for his profession: honesty, truth and vision.[138] He is one of the very few Bolsheviks in the Don region truly concerned about the Cossacks, and he opposes any drastic measures that would antagonize them. He is virtually alone in supporting Migulin and

refusing to consider him guilty prior to the trial. In the estimation of the
mature Letunov, Uncle Shura was a rare man who managed to look at the
present from the perspective of the future:

> When you float in lava, you do not notice the heat. And how
> could you see time, when you are part of it? The years have gone by,
> life has gone by, and only now you begin to understand how and
> why it happened. There were very few people who saw and under-
> stood what was happening from a distance, with the mind and the
> eyes of different times. Such was Shura. Now I know it. (p. 72)

Shura is contrasted with other Bolsheviks, such as the two commanders of "the Steel Division," Braslavsky and Shegontsev, who send hun-
dreds of hostages and suspected peasants to their deaths. Braslavsky, an
ex-worker, seems to take pleasure in avenging the killing of his family in
the pogrom of 1905, while Shegontsev firmly believes that the good of
the revolution justifies any drastic means. Characteristically, he is also
convinced that the only salvation for humankind lies in the renunciation
of feelings and emotions.

Whereas the years 1915-20 are portrayed rather extensively in the
novel, the remaining five decades are discussed very briefly, usually in
relation to other events fleetingly reconstructed by Letunov. The 1920s
are mentioned in connection with Letunov's marriage to Galya, and with
their subsequent moves from one construction site to another, necessi-
tated by his work as an engineer. Similarly, the 1930s appear sporadically
in events typical of that decade: first, a charge of sabotage, which, fortunately for Letunov, ended harmlessly, and, second, his arrest in 1935, followed by a five-year exile. The first event is recalled in connection with
Letunov's Civil War acquaintance Chevgun, who gave him wise advice in
1932, while the latter event is mentioned when Letunov thinks of his
boyhood friend Volodya and his "minute of weakness" in 1916:

> Everyone had it. I had it too. A moment of fear, not physical, not
> a fear of death, but a moment of darkness and wretchedness. A
> moment of compromise. Or perhaps, a moment of self-knowledge.
> And afterward one says: I was weak before you once, but I'll never
> give in again. It happened in 1928, no, in 1935. Galya said: "I feel
> extremely sorry for you. You didn't say it. I said it, our children said
> it." She thought everything was done because of them. (p. 34)

All in all, only one paragraph is devoted to such a crucial event, while
the exile itself is not depicted at all. The reader simply learns about

Letunov's return from exile in 1940 and the problems resulting from his loss of the right to live in Moscow. Denounced by his neighbor Prikhodko, Letunov had escaped a second arrest only because of the outbreak of the Second World War. He fought until the end of the war in the rank of private, was wounded twice, and returned to Sokolinyi Bor in 1945. All of this is mentioned laconically on less than a page, as Letunov reflects on his complex relationship with Prikkhodko while on the way to see him.

The next two decades are absent altogether, and the 1960s reappear briefly in connection with Letunov's attempts to rehabilitate Migulin. The reader learns about Letunov's work in the archives, his trips to Rostov, and his article about Migulin, which appears in 1968. Letunov's involvement in Migulin's case continues into the 1970s and is strengthened by his correspondence with Asya in the summer and fall of 1974, thus bringing the action into the present.

Past and present are closely interwoven in the novel. The present depicts actual events as they unfold from one day to the next, while the past appears almost exclusively in Letunov's recollections. All of Letunov's ventures into the past are carefully motivated. Thus, Asya's initial letter serves to set Letunov's memory in motion. In a sense, all of his reminiscences emerge in response to that letter, elaborating upon the details contained in it. Asya's second letter, on the other hand, forces Letunov to argue with her version of the crucial events of August 1919. As Migulin's former mistress, Asya remembers him mainly in terms of her feelings, speaking about his bad temper and jealousy, his mistrust of people, and his loneliness. Letunov, by contrast, tries to understand Migulin's political stand and hopes that objective documents will provide an answer. The file "Everything about Migulin" reappears several times in the novel, each time providing solace for the restless protagonist, who fights against time in his search for the truth.

Frequently, the weather stimulates Letunov's memory: a hot summer night in 1974 reminds him of the events of August 1919; a gloomy November day turns his mind to Migulin's degradation in 1920 and his own return from exile twenty years later. On other occasions a thought about a person brings back memories of that person in different times and circumstances. On his way to see Prikhodko, Letunov remembers fateful meetings with him in 1924, when he voted to exclude him from the Party, and again in 1940, when Prikhodko in turn denounced him for staying illegally in Sokolinyi Bor. Similarly, while recalling a conversation with Chevgun in 1919, Letunov remembers his wise advice some twenty years later. Occasionally, a memory of a powerful experience suggests an analogy: the details of his mother's death in the winter of 1918 evoke a comparison with the death of his wife fifty years later. In all of the above examples, there are considerable leaps in time. This lack of chronological order in the novel is motivated by the narrative structure, which reproduces the hero's thoughts and feelings in a stream of consciousness manner. Returning to the past, Letunov does not recall the events chronologically, but as separate occurrences brought together by memory associations.

Although he acts as the main narrator, Letunov cannot be completely trusted; first, because of his lapses in memory—he suffers from sclerosis, frequently forgetting details of everyday life—and second, because of his biased, one-sided interpretation of what he has witnessed. His long-range memory seems far better, but there is no doubt that he offers a highly subjective interpretation of events and people. For that very reason the narrative includes several other points of view, most notably those of Asya, Izvarin and Kandaurov, each of which adds a new perspective. A similar function is performed by the documents discussed earlier.

Despite these different narrative perspectives, the novel never clearly answers the main question of the real motives for Migulin's unauthorized leave and his subsequent intentions. What the novel does succeed in doing is to give an accurate illumination of the character of the "Old Man." The reader watches the development of his character from a naive boy at the beginning of the Revolution, through the harsh experiences of the Civil War, to a wise man in the mid-seventies. Throughout these years, Letunov remains faithful to the ideals of his uncle. Although, like many others, he has "a minute of weakness" at the time of his arrest, he returns from exile unbroken in spirit, and continues to set high moral standards for others, thus showing that honesty and compassion can guide men's lives under any circumstances. Yet he fails to pass on his high principles to his own children and grandchildren. His son Ruska appears as an irresponsible man, unable to hold on to a job and to maintain a happy marriage. Ruska's son Garik displays a shocking streak of cruelty when, in a climactic scene of killing stray dogs, he calls for the destruction of his own dog Arapka.[139]

For this reason, many Soviet critics have accused Trifonov of weakening the positive tendencies of contemporary life. Such was the opinion of Mikhail Sinelnikov, who wrote in *Voprosy literatury*: "The debilitation of real goodness is the main shortcoming in the depiction of life reconstructed in *The Old Man* in both temporal layers."[140] A similar view was given by V. Khmara: "Faith and lack of faith in the novel have different possibilities. What occurs is not so much a violation of truth as its weakening. The lack of faith that caused Migulin's downfall is transformed from historical tragedy into a much less historical and flat Evil."[141]

The opinions of the Soviet critics seem too prejudicial with regard to the implications of *The Old Man:* the novel does convey an idea of the continuity and the importance of history for the present. *The Old Man* ends with an epilogue depicting the arrival in Sokolinyi Bor of a young Ph.D. student from Rostov, a year after the death of Letunov. The student is writing about Migulin, and hopes to acquire Letunov's file. He does obtain it and is convinced that he will be able to decipher the complexities of the past: "There are times when truth and faith are joined inseparably, making it difficult to figure out what is what, but we will figure it out." (p. 209)

Thus, the novel ends on an optimistic note, postulating that the next generation will reassess the past, making it relevant for the present. The ending of *The Old Man* follows up on the two layers of the novel, adding the dimension of the future. The future tense, used by the student, emphasizes the idea of continuity and permanence, making the novel fully acceptable within the standards of Socialist Realism, which at the time still governed the development of Soviet Literature.

CHAPTER X

SHORT STORIES OF THE 1970s:

THE OVERTURNED HOUSE

The Old Man was the last of Trifonov's works to appear in his lifetime. His two novels *Time and Place* and *Disappearance* and his series of short stories entitled *The Overturned House* were published posthumously.[142] Inspired by Trifonov's foreign travel, the six stories that comprise *The Overturned House* share a common theme as well as a complex compositional and temporal structure. Like *The Old Man* these stories skillfully combine different dimensions of time and place; the impressions from foreign trips undertaken by Trifonov in the late 1970s are interwoven with his memories of people and events taking place in Russia during the preceding fifty years.

Superficially, foreign impressions occupy the predominant place in the stories: they not only provide the exotic background, but constitute the basic plot and move the action. The plot of "Cats or Rabbits?" (Koshki ili zaitsy?) revolves around the changes in the narrator, who returns to Italy after an eighteen-year absence; "Death in Sicily" (Smert' v Sitsilii) depicts his perception of this enigmatic island. The action of "Eternal Themes" (Vechnye temy) also takes place in Italy: a meeting with the former editor of an important Soviet magazine is set against the background of "the eternal city" of Rome. All three stories convey the local color of Italy by describing the geographic and climatic peculiarities: the unbearable heat in summertime Rome, the constant sound of the sea and the smell of fish in Sicily, as well as the unique qualities of the people and their habits: cheerfulness and friendliness, garrulity, and the tendency to be late.

But in all these stories the emphasis is on the narrator's subjective perception and on the analysis of his emotions. In "Cats or Rabbits?" the reader learns a great deal about the changes that have taken place in the narrator during the past two decades: from a vigorous and inquisitive man he has changed into an indifferent and apathetic observer. Moreover, he has lost his sense of surprise, which has affected his writing. Even the great shock of learning that the owner of a local restaurant, whom he extolled in an earlier story, has been accused of serving cats instead of rabbits is not enough to make him re-write the story.

The change in the narrator is also emphasized in "Eternal Themes," which contrasts a writer's youthful naiveté and insecurity with his present-day confidence. But the story is as much concerned with the transformation of the other protagonist, the once influential editor of a Soviet magazine, who has turned into a pitiful emigre. "Eternal Themes" clearly juxtaposes two different settings in time and place: the intricate literary life in Moscow in the mid-fifties and the meeting of the two protagonists twenty-two years later in Rome. The action moves back and forth between these two settings, underlining the differences between the two sets of circumstances and within the men themselves. The past appears as an indispensable part of the plot; without it the story would lose its meaning.

The same important role is played by the past in "Death in Sicily," in which life in a small Sicilian town in the late 1970s is contrasted with the events of the Civil War in Southern Russian fifty years earlier. These two distant locales and times are brought together in the life of a Russian emigre who left Russia in the early 1920s, lived in Salonica, Berlin and Paris, and, after marrying a wealthy Italian shipowner in 1945, moved to Sicily. Unlike the emigre in "Eternal Themes," Margarita Maddaloni seems well-adjusted to life. She is rich and successful, having inherited her husband's wealth and established herself as a writer of thrillers. Yet inside she is desolate, dreading death in Sicily. She admits to the narrator:

> "My dear," Senora Maddaloni covers my hand with her dry palm, "your father was on the other side. And your uncle, the commandant of Novocherkassk, perhaps persecuted my brother. That is all history. And it is of interest to very few people—you, me. . . But do you know what is the most dreadful thing?" She looks deep into me with her penetrating, frail eyes. "Death in Sicily. . ." (p. 68)

Like the other Italian stories, "Death in Sicily" reveals a great deal about the narrator, depicting his perception of the island, as well as his anxiety over the Mondello literary prize, which will be awarded to the author of the best foreign book. The narrator mentions the Italian publication of his two books: the trilogy *The Long Goodbye* and *The House on the Embankment*, thus openly identifying himself with Trifonov.

The autobiographical references are not restricted to "Death in Sicily"; they appear throughout the series. In addition to frequent mentions of his books, Trifonov incorporates many facts from his life into the stories: his early childhood in Finland, his work in a factory during the war years ("The Gray Sky, Masts and a Chestnut Horse"), his first marriage and the early death of his wife ("Visiting Marc Chagall"), his addiction to card playing ("The Overturned House"), and his frequent visits abroad. Actually, all the trips depicted in the stories are based on Trifonov's own travels in the 1970s, to Italy and the United States in 1978, to Finland and France in 1979.

Of all the stories in the series, "The Gray Sky, Masts and a Chestnut Horse" (Seroe nebo, machty, i seraia loshad') is the most autobiographical. The trip to Finland triggered memories of his early childhood in that country, where his father had worked as a Soviet trade representative. The temporal and causal distance is overwhelming: the narrator recollects details that he had registered as a small child fifty-two years earlier. His blurry memories are confirmed by a woman who had worked in the Soviet trade mission in the 1920s. In addition to recalling details from 1927, the narrator recollects some episodes connected with Finland from the next two decades: a story about three Finnish knives which Trifonov inherited after his father's arrest in 1936, and a story concerning the disappearance of his Finnish skis during the war years.

As in the other stories of this series, the past is interwoven with the present impressions of the narrator during his visit to Finland in the late 1970s. The narrator describes his short stay in Jyvaskyla, celebrating the winter carnival, and his stay in Helsinki, where he meets with his readers and veterans of the Finnish revolution. The stories told by the veterans move the action back to the year 1917, expanding the temporal framework to more than six decades and re-emphasizing the importance of the past in understanding the present.

The time span of "Visiting Marc Chagall" (Posechchenie Marka Shagala) is just as impressive, covering almost seven decades: from an exciting bohemian life in Paris in 1910 to the late 1970s in St. Paul. Contrary to the reader's expectations, the story is not focused on the famous Russian-born artist, but on the unknown Soviet painter Iona Alexandrovich, whose early friendship with Chagall haunted him throughout his life. Iona Alexandrovich's story is told by the narrator, his former son-in-law, who is on his way to visit Marc Chagall. Because of close family ties, the narrator knows a great deal about Iona; he discloses this to the reader in a fragmented and abrupt manner which reflects the way his memory works. Thus, the reader learns about Iona's last days at an old people's home in the 1970s before learning of his difficulties in trying to regain a stolen self-portrait of Chagall in the mid-1950s, or his difficulties in the early 1930s, when he was accused of "Chagallism," which, according to the narrator, "sounded like something between Shamanism and cannibalism." The emphasis in the recollections is on Iona's devotion to Chagall, whom he had always admired and defended even during the most difficult times.

The story of Iona overshadows the meeting with Chagall, which the narrator reports with painstaking accuracy. The narrator faithfully reproduces Chagall's endless questions and comments, including a remark he makes about an old painting:

> "How unhappy you have to be to paint something like this . . ."
> I thought: he has mumbled the basic truth. To be unhappy in order to paint. Later you can feel any way you want, but first you have to be unhappy. The clock in the wooden case stands aslant. One has to overcome oblique time which sweeps people around, leaving one in Vitebsk, moving another to Paris, and someone else to Maslovka Street. . . . (p. 80)

The motif of the power of time, so important in "Visiting Marc Chagall," appears in the other stories in *The Overturned House*. In "Death in Sicily" the stormy times of the revolution drastically change the lives of Margarita and her family; the Stalinist era produces people like the callous editor in "Eternal Themes," or the brazen-faced model Afanasy in "Visiting Marc Chagall." Time leaves a clear imprint on the character of the narrator, who changes from an idealistic and naive youth to a sophisticated and perceptive middle-aged writer in "Cats or Rabbits?" and "Eternal Themes." Throughout the entire series, the narrator tries to discover the connections between past and present, present and future. In "The Gray Sky, Masts and a Chestnut Horse" he examines memories of his father in order to better understand himself, while in "The Overturned House" he examines his feelings of despair over the death of his close friend, trying to imagine life without him.

The narrator frequently reflects on problems of writing and creative art in general, underlining their capacity to overcome time and preserve it for posterity. In "Eternal Themes" he recalls his earlier stories which had transmitted his mood twenty-two years before. In "Cats or Rabbits?" he reflects on his earlier story "Memory of Genziano" (Vospominanie o Dzhentsano), which conveyed his admiration for Italy during his first visit to that country eighteen years earlier.[143] And the new perception, the narrator stresses, cannot change that mood:

> One should not correct something which is beyond correction,
> which is inaccessible to being touched—that which flows through
> us. Understandably, there is little joy in learning that something
> that once amazed you and made you happy has turned out to be
> fraud and rubbish. But, my God, the feeling of happiness was there!
> (p. 59)

Along with the recurrent motifs of time and art, the series develops the
motif of death and dying.[144] The scepter of death haunts the protagonists
of two of the Italian stories, "Death in Sicily" and "Eternal Themes."
Death takes its toll in "Visiting Marc Chagall," which portrays the deaths
of Iona Alexandrovich and his daughter. The thought of death preoccu-
pies the ninety-three-year-old Marc Chagall, who rightly assumes that
most of his old friends are dead by now. The sudden death of a close
friend inspires the narrator to write the story "The Overturned House,"
in which recollections of card playing in the small Moscow suburb of
Repikhovo are interwoven with memories of Las Vegas, the gambling
capital of the world. The story portrays Boria's untimely death, in addition to the earlier death of Sergei Timofeevich, which had prompted
Boria to say, "It will catch us some day."

Despite the recurring theme of death, the simultaneous portrayal of
moments of happiness and joy keeps the series from being overly pes-
simistic. In "Cats or Rabbits?" the narrator recollects the exuberant feelings he experienced during his visit to Italy; in "The Gray Sky, Masts and
a Chestnut Horse" he recalls tranquil memories of Finland. The stories
extol the virtues of love and friendship: the stable and happy marriages of
the narrator ("Eternal Themes"), Steve and Ruth ("The Overturned
House"), and Marc Chagall ("Visiting Marc Chagall"), as well as ties of
male friendship ("The Overturned House"). Finally, they emphasize the
importance of close bonds with one's home and country, juxtaposing the
desolation of Russian emigrants with the narrator's strong attachment to
his homeland. His devotion to his native land is best conveyed in the
image of the overturned house which haunts him during his foreign travels:

> Inside the lunar landscape, within these craters, many-storeyed
> towers, the whirling of lights in the night, something familiar hides:
> I see my house, but in an overturned position. It seems to be
> spilling, dividing into layers, being reflected in the water. When I go
> far away, I always see my overturned, shattered house. It floats in
> pieces in the water. (p. 70).

The image of home is given a more realistic description as a warm place in a cold, northern land in the story "Eternal Themes." The difference between a homeless emigre and the narrator is emphasized:

> One home was far away, in the north; it was cold there now, the roads were blowing over with snow; in the morning it was necessary to call out a snowplough and the warmth was escaping through the roof like white steam. (p. 63)

Different associations are stirred by the sight of nocturnal Las Vegas, shining like a golden nugget: "A golden nugget jumped out of the darkness: Las Vegas appeared. Below flowed the blackness of the desert" (p. 69). Elsewhere in the story the city is depicted in terms of a lunar landscape, with silverish towers, craters between skyscrapers, and a white dawn. The landscape is contrasted with the agitating passion experienced by people who come to Las Vegas to gamble: "the tunnel for passengers is lined with a blood-red carpet, and at once there is a flow of languorous arousal: blood, fever, passion." The story introduces several more startling images, such as "death is a whirlwind, acting with lightning speed" (p. 71), "gambling machines—one-armed bandits" (p. 69), a semicircle of two hundred dancers, lifting their bare legs and bringing to mind "a gigantic eye-lid with white lashes" (p. 74).

The monotony of narration in the entire series of stories is broken by metaphoric descriptions of the landscape and surrounding objects. The narrator favors the device of animation, which endows inanimate objects with life and movement: "the air quivered from the heat" (p. 59), window blinds, "eliciting the impression of an unknown living creature, perhaps a mysterious fish" (p. 63), and "a winding road which would either dive into intensely hot ravines between the hills, or burst out into the freedom of a mountain top" (p. 75). Sometimes, the opposite process takes place, when a human face is compared to "a deserted old square at twilight" (p. 62), or when Boria's sudden death is perceived as "a bolt that fell out from a slot while in full motion and at mid-journey, and everything that was around—people, books, cars and pills—was spilled, flying in all directions" (p. 71). The metaphoric style of *The Overturned House* sets it apart from Trifonov's stories of the 1960s, and brings it closer to his first works in this genre.[145] Like the exotic setting of Turkmenia, foreign places provided the narrator with fresh impressions that could be transmitted in a colorful and vibrant language.

Unlike the earlier stories, the last series contains elements of irony, especially in regard to the process of creative writing and literary criticism. In "Death in Sicily" the narrator mocks the notion of the death of the novel:

> When writers get together for discussions on elevated topics,
> such as, for example, what is art and what is its purpose, they usually
> say what is generally known. The rare, precious thoughts they all
> have they tend to save for putting down on paper. I also spoke of
> the generally obvious—the novel has not died and will never do so.
> The writers of the 50s, 60s, and 70s have always defended the novel
> at their meetings; this is a kind of writers' prayer, mandatory, like
> the Catholic bedtime "Pater Noster," and I decided not to lag
> behind. Having no clear idea of who exactly attacks the novel and
> threatens it with doom, I, nevertheless, firmly and unequivocally
> warned the villains that they would not succeed. The novel will live!
> It cannot be allowed to disappear! What would people do in
> between TV programs? (p. 64)

At the same meeting the narrator draws an analogy between the novel
and the oil crisis, declaring that unlike oil, which is disappearing from the
earth, the human imagination will never run dry.

In "Eternal Themes" the irony is directed toward the biased decisions
of literary editors, who cannot even properly explain their evaluative procedures. Having rejected the narrator's short stories for their topic of
"eternal themes," the editor of an important Soviet magazine refuses to
elaborate and replies to the author:

> "Don't pretend. You know very well what I am talking about."
> "I don't know. Explain for God's sake."
> "Come on! There is nothing to explain."
> "But I actually do not understand."
> "What is there to not understand?" The man shrugged his shoul-
> ders. He looked bored, scornful. Eternal themes are eternal themes.
> But if you want... Let's say... (p. 60)

Subtle irony occurs in "The Overturned House" when an American
reader reproaches the narrator for portraying weak and indecisive heroes
who don't know how to achieve their goals:

> You see, Yury, we Americans don't like such people. We like peo-
> ple who succeed. And you Russians always write about losers. This
> is not interesting for us. We like an optimistic, life-asserting litera-
> ture. (p. 73)

Ironically, his words sound like the demands of official Soviet critics who require literature to portray positive heroes and positive values. Trifonov himself was frequently criticized for his negative approach, and in "The Gray Sky, Masts and a Chestnut Horse," he suggested a unique revenge: "For bad reviews I bought a portable paper-cutting machine; it shreds paper into the tiniest strips." (p. 82)

That machine was of no use for the reviews of *The Overturned House*, which were, without exception, positive. M. Amlinsky applauded the stories for their "condensation of thoughts, feelings and movement, not so much external, as internal, in a small form, capacious and lapidary."[146] M. Zolotonosov praised Trifonov for his method of "immersion into memory" and his exposure of "the bond between times":

> Trifonov was frequently accused of being a pessimist, of not showing confirming, positive aspects. But there was a positive tendency in all his works, expressed not in images of positive characters, as it is usually done, but in the search for the correlation of time, in the belief that everything is related to everything, yesterday to today, and today to tomorrow.[147]

Indeed in all his mature works, starting with *Reflection of the Fire* and ending with *Disappearance*, Trifonov concentrated on the links between an individual and history, the past and present, death and immortality. He succeeded in proving what Sergei Troitsky had always dreamt about:

> that the individual is the thread stretching through time, the supersensitive nerve of history that can be teased out and separated—and from which one can then learn a great deal. Man is never reconciled with death, because implanted in him is a sense that the thread of which he forms a part is endless. It is not God who rewards man with immortality, nor is the concept of immortality instilled into him by religion, but by that innate, genetically coded awareness of being a link in the infinite chain.[148]

CHAPTER XI

TIME AND PLACE:
A NOVEL IN THIRTEEN CHAPTERS

Published posthumously in 1981, *Time and Place: A Novel in Thirteen Chapters* is not only Trifonov's last completed work, but also the most complex.[149] Its complexity results from the compression of vast epic material covering a span of nearly fifty years, and the introduction of a multitude of characters and events into a narrow frame of thirteen chapters, narrated by two narrators whose voices are not always clearly distinguishable.

In an interview with the East German scholar Rulf Schroeder,[150] Trifonov used the word "punktir" [dotted line] to characterize his novel's structure: each chapter can function as an independent novella but is at the same time closely connected with the others, not only by the images, but also by the chain of time.[151] Indeed, fragmentation is the dominant feature in the compositional structure of the novel; events unfold casually and abruptly without any transition from one chapter to another, leaving the reader to wonder what has happened in the meantime.

The novel consists of thirteen chapters, a fact significant enough to Trifonov for him to place it in the subtitle. Why thirteen? The Soviet critic Bocharov dismisses any allusion to the traditional number for bad luck, citing as support for his view the central character's inner strength and the novel's happy ending.[152] But he overlooks the tragic connotations of the novel, which depicts the cruel Stalinist purges and their effects on the fates and works of Soviet writers of two generations. In addition, the novel portrays the anguish of writing, illustrated by the work of the hero Antipov, his teacher Kiyanov, and his colleagues from the Literary

Institute.

The thirteen chapters are, as a rule, loosely connected to each other; the time and frequently the place of action change abruptly. Between the first chapter, which depicts the summer of 1937 in a small resort near Moscow, and the last one, portraying the winter of 1980, runs a succession of different years, places and people. The chapters are united by the figure of Sasha Antipov, who develops from an innocent boy of eleven to a mature writer in the 1960s and 1970s. Antipov's life constitutes the major plot line in the novel, taking up three-quarters of the entire narrative.

A second, parallel line comprises the reminiscences of the nameless author-narrator,[153] who recollects some facts about Sasha as well as his own childhood and youth. These two lines seldom cross each other in the novel and are transmitted in totally different narrative voices. Whereas the author-narrator speaks in the first person, Antipov's voice is conveyed in a third-person narrative which reproduces his point of view. What at first seems to be an "objective" authorial narrative turns out to be a subjective personal account of events, thoughts and feelings. In contrast, the author-narrator's seemingly personal voice proves to be a dispassionate account of others with very little information about his own self.

The second significant difference between the two narrative voices stems from the divergent temporal structures. Whereas the author-narrator uses a distinctive past tense to convey his recollections of the past, the story of Antipov unfolds in the narrative present, displaying the events to the reader as they happen. This is not to say that the narrative transmitting Antipov's point of view is always in the grammatical present tense; on the contrary, many chapters are written in the past, but they all develop the plot in a chronologically ordered direction. In contrast, the chapters written by the author-narrator do not advance the plot but investigate the past from a double perspective—the viewpoint of the narrator both at a given age and as a mature man recollecting his childhood and youth. Characteristically, all the reminiscences are brought eventually to the present, illustrating the reaction and attitude of the narrator toward the events and people described earlier.

The two lines are not assigned an equal role in the novel's structure. Whereas the story of Antipov is undoubtedly the central one, the reminiscences of the author-narrator constitute a subplot which conveys the idea of the victory of man over time owing to his capacity for memory, his ability to conquer the ephemeral, transitory nature of experience by fixing it in memory.[154]

The novel opens with a prologue posing the question of the value of human memory. The narrator sketches a few details from Sasha's childhood and simultaneously asks a question: "Should one remember those events and people, those places and times?" Although the initial answer is negative, the novel proceeds to depict Sasha and his friends playfully swimming in the Moscow river on a bright August morning. The reader immediately notices the change in narrative voice from the serious tone of author-narrator to the innocent expression of an eleven-year-old boy who recounts his summer experiences, oblivious to events in the outside world. The chapter ends with Sasha's sudden departure. He says good-bye to the river, fields and a white cloud. The lyrical mood aroused by this scene continues into the last paragraph, which returns to the question posed in the prologue. By this time the answer is positive:

> Should one remember? My God, it is as foolish as asking: should one live? After all, to remember and to live is part of the same process; neither one can be destroyed without the other, and together they form a certain verb which has no name. (p. 77)

Having established that important fact, the author-narrator moves on to recall some events from his childhood and youth: his friendship with Lyovka Gordeev, his first love for Ola Pletneva, and his work with Sasha Antipov during the war. He discloses very little about himself, speaking mainly of others: the Gordeev family in chapter 2, the three generations of Pletnev women in chapter 5, and his co-workers in the Aircraft Factory in chapter 6. Moreover, his own identity remains unclear until chapter 6, at first making it possible for the reader to mistake him for the adult Antipov. The narrator recollects his parentless childhood in Moscow at the end of the 1930s and his work in a factory during the war. The differentiation between the two becomes apparent only in chapter 6, in which the narrator depicts Sasha as a co-worker in the factory, and speaks of the great resemblance between them:

> We both wore glasses, and were slow and quiet. . . . We both were of the same age, I being half a year younger. We both lived without our parents, I with my grandmother, and he with his older sister and his aunt. Like me, he dabbled in writing and dreamed of studying in the Literary Institute after the war. (p. 121)

Brought together by the war, the narrator and Sasha went separate ways for the next thirty-five years until life brings them together again when their children accidentally meet. In the last chapter of the novel, or more precisely in the epilogue, the narrator describes that meeting and the feeling of closeness which prevails despite the separation of years. The epilogue illustrates the similarities in fate and outlook of both men, depicting them as typical representatives of the whole generation.

All in all, the author-narrator acts as the sole storyteller in four chapters, with short appearances in the prologue and at the end of chapter 1 and the beginning of chapter 3. Typically for the technique which Trifonov called "punktir," all the chapters have episodic natures, each depicting an event set at a different time and place with different characters. Moreover, there is no clear connection between the chapters, except for the figures of Antipov and the enigmatic narrator. The reader learns very little about the narrator, however, and has to construct his biography on the basis of extremely scarce information —his parentless childhood in pre-war Moscow, his work in a factory during the war, his research at the Institute of Mathematics, the early death of his wife, and his raising of a daughter. Some of these details correspond to Trifonov's own biography, but on the whole, the writer seems to separate himself from the narrator.[155]

There is more similarity between the writer and the novel's hero, who shares with Trifonov the profession of writer, studies at the Literary Institute, lives first on Kaluzhskaya street and later near the airport, and has a child late in life. Antipov appears as a "concealed" narrator in nine chapters. He reveals a great deal about himself, not through stream-of-consciousness probes into his inner self, but through his perception of events and people. Like the author-narrator, Antipov is extremely selective in his choice of material. He concentrates on the major events in his life, leaving long periods of time unexplored, about which the reader can merely speculate. From the first chapter, depicting the eleven-year-old boy, the action jumps in chapter 3 to the year 1946, when at age twenty he learns about the past directly from his mother, who has just returned from an eight-year exile. Antipov is not so much interested in the political implications of what he hears as in its potential literary usefulness. As a student in the Literary Institute he is looking for the "right" material for his work.

A great deal of attention is devoted to the next few years in Antipov's life, the formative period in his writing career and in his personal life. Chapters 4 and 7 depict the torments of a beginning writer, combined with the sexual torments of a celibate youth. He experiences his first platonic love and then his first physical encounter. The crucial year of 1947 ends for Antipov with mixed success: he publishes his first story, but loses his beloved Natasha, who retreats to a Kuban village after her lover is killed. Chapter 8 continues to explore the anxieties of creative writing; Antipov rewrites his first novel, and faces a moral dilemma at the trial of a manager of a small publishing house who is accused of plagiarism. Faced with the choice of pleasing his editor and securing the publication of his book, or testifying according to his conscience, he chooses the latter, thus proving to himself and to others that the correct moral stand is more important than personal gain.

There are short glimpses of Antipov's life during the next decade in chapter 9, which depicts his agony over the planned abortion, and in chapter 10, where he is shown as an intermediary between the writers' union and his ex-professor Kiyanov. Then the reader loses track of Antipov for more than ten years. We meet him again at the moment of his next personal crisis—his marriage of twenty years is falling apart and he is experiencing difficulties in revising his major novel *Nikiforov's Syndrome*. Chapter 11, the longest in the novel, portrays in great detail the complexities of the creative process and the sufferings of a writer struggling unsuccessfully to transmit his ideas.

The last chapter, reflecting Antipov's point of view, catches him at another critical moment. Alone in a rented room (he had left his family five years earlier), he suffers a heart attack, and as he is carried down the stairs, he contemplates:

> . . . there was no time better than the one he had lived through. And there is no place better than these stairs with broken paint on the wall, with water stains above, with some pencil graffiti, with the voices and smells of life, with an open window behind which stirred the fiery glow of the city night. (p. 101)

What appears to be the last moment of Antipov's life proves otherwise after one reads the last chapter of the novel, written by the author-narrator. The reader learns of Antipov's recovery, his second marriage and a late-born son, and of his teaching career at the Literary Institute. His life seems to make a full circle: from a student in that Institute to a teacher passing the secrets of his profession on to the next generation of writers.

The chapters transmitting Antipov's point of view are on the whole as abrupt as those written by the narrator. In addition to large temporal gaps between chapters, there are sudden changes of place and circumstance. Unlike the narrator, Antipov is shown not only in familiar Moscow surroundings but also against the background of Kuban, Mongolia and Czechoslovakia. It is significant that, although he leaves Moscow during various crises, he always returns to it. Moscow becomes the symbol of a permanent home, a place to which one can always return and start anew.[156]

In addition to the two main narrators discussed above, *Time and Place* also offers the narrative voices of other characters in the novel, most notably the old woman Pletneva and the writer Kiyanov. The former, who offers her reminiscences of the pre-revolutionary struggle and exile in chapter 5, deviates from the main story line, but the latter, whose diary is reproduced in chapter 10, strengthens an important theme of the novel—that of the anxieties of creative writing and the unavoidable compromises that a writer has to make. Pletneva is a minor character, appearing only in one chapter, whereas Kiyanov is one of the novel's major characters, first depicted through the eyes of Antipov, his student in the Literary Institute, and then given an independent voice which reveals the insight of a man and a writer. The intimate portrait of Kiyanov that emerges from his diary only confirms the characterization provided by Antipov: a talented writer, crushed by circumstances and unable to produce anything new. Kiyanov's diary elucidates the most crucial period in his life—the purges of the 1930s. The apolitical stand he took saved his life but destroyed his inner strength.

Written in August 1957, after the return from exile of his friend Misha Teterin, the diary goes back to the 1920s and 1930s, and describes their joint publication of the journal *Prichal*, the attacks upon it in 1928, the appearance of Teterin's book *Aquarium* in 1934 and the campaign to discredit it. The diary concentrates on Kiyanov's crucial meeting with Misha the night before his arrest, when Misha asked Kiyanov to withdraw his name from the play they wrote together in order to save its future. Kiyanov acts accordingly, but twenty years later, he still feels uneasy about it and tries to justify his action to himself. At this point, the reader is prompted to believe Kiyanov, and perhaps even to feel compassion for this sixty-three-year-old man, troubled by his conscience and trying to understand why Misha avoids him after exile. But the subsequent developments, depicted in the same chapter, seem to contradict the interpretation of events Kiyanov provides, first of all by relating the case against Kiyanov which Teterin's second wife initiates, and, secondly, by introducing Teterin's denial of the 1938 meeting. The chapter ends when Kiyanov dies from an overdose of medication. Is it an accident or a premeditated act? Depending on the version the reader chooses to believe, Kiyanov appears either as a villain taking advantage of his friend, or simply a weak man, unable to take a firm stand and afraid of reality.

The strength of the latter interpretation is supported by Kiyanov's recurrent dream, which is reproduced in the same chapter: he stands in a huge deserted shelter-like place, watching a crowd of bare-footed people dressed in white who are running past him and paralyzing him with fear. Kiyanov is likewise paralyzed by fear in real life—he tries to avoid controversial issues and remain totally "apolitical." This fear costs him a high price as a writer: his major novel is a failure and he is unable to write anything new.

Kiyanov's desolate life is not only depicted in the novel directly, but also indirectly; he is cast in the role of the protagonist in Antipov's work *Nikiforov's Syndrome,* which portrays a middle-aged, unsuccessful writer who tries to recreate the "unaccomplished" life of another writer. Eventually, *Nikiforov's Syndrome* turns into a complicated novel, depicting in a system of mirrors going back two centuries the attempts of five different writers to write about their unsuccessful predecessors. Unlike Antipov's other works, *Nikiforov's Syndrome* is described in *Time and Place* with great care; the details of its theme and characters are disclosed and long quotations from it appear. It becomes a classic example of a novel within a novel, illustrating the secrets of creative art and the process of transformation of reality into fiction.[157]

Intended as Antipov's major opus, *Nikiforov's Syndrome* turns into a failure, rejected by editors and criticized by reviewers. But Antipov does not give up on his novel. He rewrites it for three years and at one point begins it anew. He compares his work to a painful "self-operation," suggesting an analogy between Nikiforov-Kiyanov and himself. He suffers from the same syndrome as his teacher —the fear of reality—but knows that only by suppressing this fear can he accomplish his work as a writer. Antipov reveals to his mother:

> I did not succeed [with the novel], probably because I began something which is beyond my strength. I am not capable of sufficiently drawing things out. And it is necessary. To draw upon the last drop, to the very bottom; I understood this towards the end, when it was too late. But it's not important. Don't worry. I'll write something that will be good. (p. 94)

The reader never learns about the fate of Antipov's *Nikiforov's Syndrome,* or about his other works mentioned earlier in the novel. Likewise, the novel does not provide answers to such questions as what became of Antipov's literary career after *Nikiforov's Syndrome,* why he left his family, or what was the nature of his second marriage and his life after the heart attack. There are even more unanswered questions concerning the author-narrator, who is characterized only by a few details from his boyhood and youth, but whose adult life is surrounded by a cloud of mystery.

On the whole, *Time and Place* is marked by a great deal of reticence, which prompted two Soviet critics to remark: "In the composition of the novel an important role is played not only by the chapters (text), but also by the blank spaces separating the chapters from one another."[158] Indeed, the large time lapses between many chapters obscure long periods in the lives of both narrators, forcing the reader to create his own picture of their actions and inner development.

These gaps are the result of the open structure of the novel, which introduces selected episodes from the life of the hero without making connections. It is exactly what Trifonov had in mind when he used the word "punktir" to describe his novel: it consists of a series of episodes, each of which may be considered as an independent whole and at the same time may be a part in the overall time chain of events.

Time and Place has an open ending consistent with its structure; the action stops at a seemingly randomly chosen moment when major conflicts are not resolved. The novel could easily have been extended to elucidate the future of Antipov and the narrator. As it stands, the ending simply brings the two story lines together, thus underlining the importance of both for the structure of the novel. First of all, the interplay of the story lines helps to fill the temporal gaps resulting from the abrupt jumps between the chapters. Thus, the narrator's reminiscences provide information about the years missing from Antipov's story: the end of the 1930s, the war years, and the end of the 1970s. Secondly, due to the similarities in the lives of both narrators, their two story lines emphasize the idea of the common fate of their whole generation. Thirdly, they both point, each in a different way, to the idea of man conquering time: through memory, in the case of the author-narrator, and through creative writing, in the case of Antipov and other writers in the novel.

Despite all the differences, the two story lines complement each other both in their temporal and ideological structures. Thanks to the two lines, the novel transmits an important message: life is restricted by time and place, but there is a way to overcome these restrictions through the aid of memory and the creative process. Paraphrasing the words of the narrator on the inseparability of life and memory, one can add: "to create and to live is part of the same process, one cannot be destroyed without the other, and together they create a verb which has no name."

CHAPTER XII

DISAPPEARANCE

Six years after Trifonov's death, the journal *Druzhba narodov* published his unfinished novel *Disappearance* (Ischeznovenie).[159] According to the introductory note by the writer's widow, Olga Trifonova-Miroshnichenko, he had been working on this novel for more than two decades, from the late 1950s, when he was writing *The Quenching of Thirst*, to the 1970s, when he was composing *The House on the Embankment, The Old Man,* and *Time and Place.* Olga Trifonova compares *Disappearance* to a diary, or a notebook in which a writer records his most important thoughts. Although the comparison is misleading, since *Disappearance* has all the qualities of a novel, the introductory remarks help to explain the work's strong autobiographical aspect and its similarity to Trifonov's earlier novels.

The autobiographical material introduced in the novel deals with two important periods in Trifonov's life: his childhood years in "the house on the embankment" in the late 1930s and his evacuation to Tashkent in 1941. The life of the novel's hero, Gorik Bayukov, closely follows Trifonov's own experiences and those of his family and friends. Thus, the portraits of Gorik's father, Nikolai Grigorevich, and his brother Mikhail bear a striking resemblance to Valentin and Evgeny Trifonov in the years before the Revolution and during the 1930s. Similarly, the image of Gorik's grandmother is modeled after Trifonov's maternal grandmother, Tatyana Alexandrovna Slovatinskaya, portraying her work in Moscow in the mid-thirties and her evacuation with two grandchildren, Yury and Zhenya, to Tashkent in 1941. The novel also depicts Trifonov's real school friends, such as Leva Fedotov, a remarkable talent who perished during World War II.160

With its strong autobiographical inclination, *Disappearance* in many ways resembles Trifonov's earlier works, most notably *Reflection of the Fire*, *The Old Man* and *Time and Place*. Like *Reflection of the Fire* and *The Old Man*, the novel sketches episodes from the Civil War which involve the work of the Military Tribunal in the Don area. But whereas in both earlier works the year 1920 was at the center of the narrative, in *Disappearance* it surfaces only briefly in the form of reminiscences by the elder Bayukov. *Disappearance* also reconstructs some events from the pre-revolutionary past of the Bayukov brothers and David Shvarts, in many ways resembling the lives of the Trifonov brothers and Aron Solts, as portrayed in *Reflection*.

Like *The House on the Embankment*, *Disappearance* portrays the events of the 1930s seen from the perspective of a young boy who senses the disturbing atmosphere but cannot understand the political reality. But whereas Vadim Glebov watched the life of the Soviet elite from the outside, Gorik Bayukov can observe it from within, since his family belongs to the establishment and he has a distinctive feeling of superiority. The Bayukovs represent idealistic and honest communists, while corruption and careerism are identified with Arseny Florinsky, a blood-brother of Shulepnikov in *The House on the Embankment*. In both novels a great deal of attention is devoted to the theme of school friendship, illustrated in *The House* by the Secret Society for Testing the Will, and in *Disappearance* by the Society for Investigating Caves and Underground Passages. In both cases the young heroes are inspired by their brilliant leaders; in *The House on the Embankment*— Anton Ovchinnikov, and in *Disappearance*—Lenya Karastyn.

In the depiction of the second temporal layer, that of World War II, *Disappearance* is similar to Trifonov's *Time and Place* in its picture of Moscow in the early 1940s. In both novels the protagonists are initially evacuated to Central Asia and return to Moscow to work in a military factory. But whereas *Time and Place* concentrates on the depiction of the work itself, *Disappearance* also portrays Igor's relations with his co-workers and relatives. It also provides a more detailed picture of life in evacuation, which is mentioned only briefly in *Time and Place*.

Although it shares many common features with Trifonov's earlier novels, *Disappearance* surpasses all of them in the detailed portrayal of the political purges in the late 1930s and the attempt to understand the mechanism behind the political terror.161 The novel depicts several instances of arrests and disappearances, involving people from totally different spheres of life, such as the engineer Nikodin, an editor of a philo-

sophical journal Volovik, the old Bolshevik Yakov Slivyansky, or the
nameless cameraman in the Mosfilm studio. Although all the above
"cases" are different, they share some common denominators—an
unfounded suspicion of the professional intelligentsia and a mistrust of
old Bolsheviks. The latter case is illustrated by the fates of David Shvarts
and Nikolai and Mikhail Bayukov, who are removed from responsible
positions and lose their political influence. The systematic demotion of
old Bolsheviks is contrasted in the novel with the sudden rise of a new
elite, associated with the secret police and embodied by Arseny Florinsky.
Rancorous and ruthless, he is a typical product of the Ezhov administration, convinced that "the most important task is to fight against the
opponents of democracy, against the enemies hiding behind party mem-
bership cards, against the pseudo-communists" (p. 38).

In addition to portraying the actual purges, the novel addresses the
question of the complacent involvement of the old Bolsheviks and their
moral responsibility for the ongoing terror. It attempts to explain what
made the idealistic Bolsheviks, like David Shvarts or Nikolai Bayukov,
accept terror and even justify it to themselves and to others. Ironically,
many of them, like Florinsky, accept Stalin's argument of the class struggle against internal enemies and against Germans. Gorik's friend Lenya
repeats his father's words: "Now is the most difficult time, even more difficult than war. Because there are enemies everywhere. Saboteurs, spies,
wreckers, double dealers, and so on" (p. 71). And Gorik's own father, the
idealistic Nikolai Grigorevich, uses the same argument to reassure Masha:
"The real cause is the fear of Fascism. Perhaps it is a German provocation.
There is no other explanation" (p. 87). Only later does Nikolai
Grigorevich recognize that it is not a German provocation, but "Russia's
own product. And with a long tradition. It is the question of power" (p.
90). Although Nikolai Grigorevich does not openly refer to Stalin, that
link is established by his brother Misha, who had already predicted in
1918: "if he takes power in his hands, he will make a mess of things" (p.
90).

Stalin's oppressive use of power is perceived by the Bayukov brothers
as "an extended iron slab, hanging in mid-air." They know it will have to
fall down one day, but are not able to do anything to hasten it. The
Bayukovs' growing awareness of the cult of Stalin is reinforced in the
novel by the image of the colossal portrait of Stalin hanging above the
Kremlin on the eve of May 1. Watching that huge portrait hanging in
mid-air on an invisible threat, the brothers perceive it as "supernatural"
and "miraculous" (p. 92).

Disappearance ends abruptly with an episode describing the First of
May celebration. The last pages register the Bayukovs' feeling of anxiety

and their premonition of their vulnerability:

> "You know, Kolya, we won't see the end of this year."
> "It is quite likely," Nikolai answered quietly, almost absentmindedly. "It is likely. But the fact is... The war will soon break out. And our internal spinning will end, and we will put on our military coats and will go to fight the Fascists." (p. 90)

Nikolai Grigorevich was right about the inevitability of war against Germany, but his brother Mikhail proved more correct in his premonition of their impending arrest. In real life, neither of the Trifonov brothers survived the year 1937; Valentin was arrested on June 22, and Evgeny died of a heart attack in December, apparently while awaiting his arrest.

Although unfinished, *Disappearance* displays a very coherent temporal and narrative structure. On the temporal level, it juxtaposes two main layers: the winter and spring of 1937 are alternated with the fall and early winter of 1942 except for the last two chapters, which depict the eve and day of May 1. Out of the eight chapters that comprise the novel three deal with the events of 1942, four with the year 1937, and one, the first chapter, is set a few decades later.

The first chapter functions in the novel not only as a philosophical statement on the flow of time and its impact on people and places, but also as a means of establishing a mature perspective on the consequent events and destinies of the characters. Despite the use of the first-person singular, the narrator's voice resembles the tone of an omniscient narrator.

The narrative point of view changes drastically in chapter 2 when the first person is replaced by a third-person narration which conveys the perspective of Igor Bayukov. This chapter tells the story of Igor's return to Moscow in October 1942, and reminisces about his evacuation to Tashkent during the past year. Acting as a "concealed" narrator,[162] Igor presents his perception of the harsh war years, offers his evaluation of events and characters, and reveals his own thoughts and feelings. He relies primarily on reported description, presenting external detail through the prism of his vision, and disclosing his emotional response. Upon his return to Moscow, for example, he registers the changes that took place in the city and communicates his simultaneous feeling of joy and sadness:

> Moscow shocked him with its silence and scantiness of people. Even at the train station there were hardly any people and the buses were quite empty; somehow it deeply moved him. He felt as if he

recognized a familiar face changed through suffering and the years of separation. (p. 15)

As a concealed narrator, Igor offers his perception of other characters and an evaluation of their behavior. As a result, they tend to be two-dimensional and flat, lacking psychological depth and individualization. This applies both to the relatives with whom Igor shares an apartment—his Aunt Dina, her daughter Marinka, and her mother Vera—as well as to his co-workers, such as Kolka, Nastya or Uryuk.

The psychological portrayal of Igor, on the other hand, is excellent. The flow of Igor's thought is conveyed in his narration, in which sense perceptions mingle with conscious and unconscious thoughts, memories and feelings. His inner turmoil in response to a call from his supervisor is depicted in this passage:

> A sudden anxiety captured him. He could only think of one explanation: it had something to do with the questionnaire. They could fire him on the spot. Or even worse, they could accuse him of hiding true facts in order to penetrate into a military factory. . . A strange indifference replaced anxiety. He walked slowly on the planked footway on the second floor, tapping the rail with his hand and thinking: "So what? I answered correctly. He died in such and such a year. That's what they told me: he died from pneumonia. And mother works in Kazakhstan in her field. She works as a live-stock expert in a sovkhoz. Nothing to it." (p. 23)

In both indirect and direct monologue Igor discloses his most intimate thoughts and feelings, allowing the reader to understand his inner state of mind.

In narrating the events of 1942, Igor works within a temporal frame-work of two months, but he actually portrays only several days: the day of his return to Moscow in October, three days in November, and a day in December. In addition, he frequently recollects some experiences from the past, most notably the summer of 1938 spent in Shabanovo, and the past year spent in evacuation in Tashkent. Almost all Igor's recollections are motivated realistically; clear indications are given as to how his mem-ory is stirred by external factors. When he looks at old pictures in Dina's apartment, he recalls the summer of 1938; his grandmother Vera's remarks about her former son-in-law, Nikodimov, make Igor remember his childish image of that man several years earlier. Similarly, a dry apricot Igor finds in an old jacket reminds him of his experiences in evacuation.

In a way one could even argue that the 1937 chapters can be seen as

Igor's recollections of his past.[163] Such an interpretation is especially valid for chapter 3, which provides a detailed description of the episode first mentioned in Igor's dream at the end of chapter 2. Another dream, depicted at the end of chapter 4, can be regarded as a transition toward the story of the Pushkin competition related in chapter 5. It is more difficult to justify the abrupt change from chapter 6 to 7, since there is no apparent connection between the episode where Igor "steals" bread and the account of the cave exploration in the spring of 1937.

There is, however, a strong argument against regarding the 1937 chapters as retrospective glances by the hero into his childhood. This argument is provided by the heterogeneous narrative structure of the second plot layer. Unlike the 1942 chapters, in which Igor was used as the only concealed narrator, the 1937 chapters rely on several narrative voices: the voice of the younger Igor, called by his childish name Gorik, and those of his father, Nikolai Grigorevich, his uncle Serezha, and their influential neighbor Florinsky. Whereas the last two are clearly secondary and act as concealed narrators only for brief moments, the voices of Gorik and his father are central, alternating and complementing each other. Dealing with the same temporal framework, they nevertheless differ in their focus and evaluation of events. As an adolescent narrator, the eleven-year-old Gorik speaks about his life in school and at home, and reports external events without understanding or correctly interpreting their significance. Nikolai Grigorevich, on the other hand, is less concerned with the events themselves than with the effect they have on his life. He is constantly analyzing his thoughts and feelings and conveying them to the reader in a form close to interior monologue.

Gorik perceives the world around him with a childish simplicity and naiveté, taking things out of their habitual context and seeing them in a new, fresh way. This technique of "estrangement" presents the habitual in a novel light.[164] Clear examples of estrangement are provided by the descriptions of the underground caves which capture Gorik's fear and uneasiness, and the picture of the May Day parade which conveys his exultant enthusiasm. More frequently, estrangement discloses Gorik's bewilderment over the strange, unreasonable behavior of adults, such as his uncle Misha's separation from his wife, or the strained relations between his grandmother and Sergei. The most interesting instances of estrangement convey Gorik's naiveté with regard to politics. Thus, he speaks of his uncle Misha's personal problems without realizing that the real cause of his misfortune lies in his demotion and his fear of arrest. In a similar way, Gorik watches his family's grave reaction to the news of Ordzhonikidze's death without grasping the consequences of that event. One of the best examples of Gorik's innocent vision is how he reports the results of the Pushkin competition in his school. Greatly disappointed that he does not win a prize, Gorik does not understand why the first prize is awarded to a statue of a young Stalin reading Pushkin, or why the most interesting exhibit, the monster's head from Pushkin's tale *Ruslan and Lyudmila,* is hastily removed from the exhibition and its creator transferred to another school.

The passages marked by estrangement, effectively used to signal the child's point of view, are occasionally supplemented by the voice of the omniscient narrator, who corrects the distorted vision of the child by providing additional information or expressing his own opinions. The voice of the omniscient narrator is heard most distinctly during moments of dramatic tension, such as Ordzhonikidze's death or the revelation that Sapozhnikov's father is a German spy. In the first instance, the omniscient narrator comments on the different careers of Ordzhonikidze and Nikolai Grigorevich:

> Later their paths went in different directions. Sergo rapidly advanced and became one of the leaders, while Nikolai Grigorevich was gradually demoted and became one of the thousands of ordinary Party workers. (p. 50)

Similarly, at the end of the chapter the omniscient narrator depicts the boys' expedition to the caves and their feeling of uneasiness upon learning about Sapozhnikov's father:

> Everything that Karas said was clear and wise, but that wisdom suddenly bored them. The time for play was coming to an end. Something else was beginning. But they did not want to believe it. For all their lives, a long one for one, a short and tragic one for another, they did not want to believe that *the time for play was over.* (p. 72)

The opinions of the omniscient narrator are also incorporated into a portrait of Gorik:

> Gorik understood that to be conceited and proud is not good, but like a smoker who craves tobacco and cannot live without it, even while knowing how bad it is, he could not function without that familiar and usual feeling of tickling pride, a pride about anything at all, constant, sometimes even subconscious. (p. 40)

The above passage clearly indicates not only the omniscient narrator's disapproval of Gorik, but also his phraseology and idiom. The comparison of Gorik's vanity to an addiction to smoking, and the metaphoric image of tickling pride clearly indicate the language of the adult omniscient narrator. Most of the narrative transmitting Gorik's point of view is rendered in this language.

It is harder to distinguish between the language of the omniscient narrator and that of Nikolai Grigorevich since both of them rely on a similar style. What helps to establish Nikolai Grigorevich's voice, however, is his constant reliance on words that relate to his perception, thoughts and feelings, that indicate his reaction to, and interpretation of, events. As a concealed narrator, he is most concerned with the impact events have on his state of mind. During Nikolai Grigorevich's visit to David Shvarts, for example, he experiences a feeling of peace and relief, then anguish:

> The feeling of peace suddenly disappeared. Nikolai Grigorevich left overwhelmed by anguish—an anguish that was not personal, not a reflection of himself, but general, vague and boundless, and therefore not subject to cure. (p. 35)

The feeling of anguish becomes even stronger at the end of the visit to Florinsky, when Nikolai Grigorevich realizes that his visit has served no purpose: "While leaving he understood that it was a vain undertaking. The vague anguish that he felt at David's took hold of him with such force that his heart ached" (p. 39).

Acting as a concealed narrator, Nikolai Grigorevich reports the events of only two days: a visit in February to Shvarts and Florinsky in order to intercede for Nikodimov, and a meeting with Masha Poluboyarova on the eve of May 1. But he recalls numerous episodes from the past, including his first encounter with David in exile in 1913, his work with Florinsky in the Don Military Tribunal in 1920, and the party purges in the 1920s and early 1930s. As with Igor's reminiscences, Nikolai Grigorevich's recollections are motivated realistically. His first recollections occur during his car ride to David's and depict their first meeting and Nikodimov's problems. The second group of recollections takes place after Nikolai receives a note from Masha. The note brings back memories of their first meeting in Rostov in 1920 and their brief encounter in 1925.

In both cases the reminiscences accentuate the theme of the revolutionary past and illustrate the old Bolsheviks' total dedication to the cause. They also refer to the ongoing party purges which began in the early 1920s and increased in the 1930s. Most importantly, however, the reminiscences help to enhance the psychological portrayal of Nikolai Grigorevich by demonstrating his idealism and moral integrity in the past and elucidating his position of uncompromising honesty in the present. Owing to the use of interior monologue, the reader can observe Nikolai Grigorevich's growing awareness of the ongoing terror and his attempts to understand the mechanism governing it. Wrong as he is in his assessment of the situation, he illustrates the high principles and incorruptibility that prevailed among some of the party members even at the height of terror.

Ironically, the image of Nikolai Grigorevich that emerges from his narrative contradicts his son's perception of him. In Gorik's eyes, his father was an all-knowing and powerful figure, but in reality Nikolai Grigorevich had lost all his influence and had become an insignificant party worker. All in all, the use of Nikolai Grigorevich as a concealed narrator strengthens the ideological connotations of the novel. Whereas a young hero could only report external events without understanding their significance, a mature narrator, himself involved in politics, can unveil the true proportions of the political terror of the 1930s.

The same motivation probably was behind the use of the secret police agent Florinsky and Nikolai Grigorevich's brother-in-law Sergei as concealed narrators. By probing into the mind of a KGB official and by introducing another example of the purges, Trifonov wanted to present a more comprehensive picture of the ongoing terror and to illustrate different attitudes to it. Yet as they stand in the novel, both Florinsky and Sergei appear superfluous and fail to bring any new dimensions to the story. The psychological portrait of Florinsky is so threadbare that it only confirms the reader's worst expectations. The story of Volovik's downfall, as described by Sergei, is yet another example of political purges typical of the 1930s.

In the opinion of some Soviet critics, *Disappearance,* with its conspicuous portrayal of the purges, had been written "for the drawer," without much hope for publication.[165] It was eventually published owing to changes in the political and cultural climate in the Soviet Union in the mid-eighties. Under "glasnost" writers were allowed to depict the repressions of the 1930s and the effects of the cult of Stalin. Immediately after publishing *Disappearance,* the journal *Druzhba narodov* serialized Anatoly Rybakov's *The Children of the Arbat,* written twenty years earlier, which chronicled the life of the largely autobiographical character Sasha Pankratov against the background of the mid-thirties.[166] A few months earlier, *Znamya* printed Alexander Bek's *The New Assignment,* which depicted the disastrous consequences of pseudo-innovations in Soviet metallurgy in the thirties and illustrated the psychology of "Stalin's soldiers."[167] In 1986 also appeared Vladimir Amlinsky's *Every Hour Will be Justified,* portraying the purges in Soviet genetics in the late 1940s through the authentic case of the author's father, Professor Ilya Amlinsky.[168]

Compared with these works, *Disappearance* stands out as the most concise, yet highly revealing, exposé of the cult of Stalin. Although unfinished, it has a remarkably tight structure in which the voices of the several narrators and the juxtaposition of several periods of time do not clash, but complement and depend on one another, creating a coherent whole. The tone of the novel is strikingly impartial and composed, but behind that tranquillity the reader can sense the tragedy pertinent to that period of "temporary insanity" which forced many people to give up their ideals and adapt themselves to changing circumstances.

CONCLUSION

In assessing the thirty-year literary career of Yury Trifonov, one can clearly see two distinct features: first, his consistent use of several prose forms—the short story, the novella and the novel; second, his gradual evolution from the strict models of Socialist Realism towards a more open psychological realism.

Trifonov made his literary debut with the novel *Students*, which closely adhered to the requirements of Socialist Realism: it portrayed an idealized student collective, governed by social and political concerns and struggling against any manifestations of individualism. In accordance with the prescribed model, characters tended to be black and white; the "positive" ones obeyed the rules of the collective, the "negative" ones were preoccupied with their own interests and ambitions. All conflicts were resolved happily: those individuals who strayed returned to the collective and worked for the betterment of the country.

Trifonov continued to rely on the traditional models of Socialist Realism in his Turkmenian stories and his novel *The Quenching of Thirst*, which glorifies the construction of the Kara-Kum canal within the conventions of an "industrial" genre. Following new developments in Soviet literature in the sixties, the theme of industrialization was combined with one of moral renewal, and attention was shifted from purely technological problems to the personal lives of the characters. Given this new focus, *The Quenching of Thirst* offered a deeper psychological portrayal of characters and a more convincing picture of Soviet reality.

The widening of thematic scope and greater attention to the psychology of the characters in *The Quenching of Thirst* marked Trifonov's first steps toward a new style of writing which he developed in the late 1960s and 1970s. In his "Moscow" novellas he established himself as an exponent of psychological realism and switched focus from the socio-political significance of events toward a psychological exploration of characters and a sensitive reproduction of their inner worlds.

During this period Trifonov proved himself a master of the novella, a genre of intermediate length and scope which expands the narrow frame of the short story through a more complicated plot, an ampler development of milieu, and more subtle exploration of characters. Trifonov's novellas are distinguished from those of his contemporaries by their consistent focus on the details of everyday life and the ethics of human relations, as well as their skillful narration. He relies on a concealed narrator who reports the subjective point of view of a character in a seemingly objective third-person singular voice with no substantial interference by the voice of an "author."

The Moscow novellas established Trifonov as one of the most popular Soviet writers. His work was widely read and discussed, and it was staged in theaters and on television. But Trifonov continued to expand his forms to convey a sense of the "time and place" which determines an individual's fate and character. Starting with *The House on the Embankment*, he supplemented the psychological investigation of his characters with an investigation of the milieu in which they lived in order to show the link between the individual and history, the past and the present, and to reflect on life and death. Furthermore, he conveyed this vast epic material in a complex novelistic form, using a complex compositional and temporal framework as well as a polyphony of narrative voices. Contrary to the strict canons of Socialist Realism, he managed to avoid a tone of omnipotence and didacticism by eliminating the authoritative voice of an omniscient narrator and forcing the readers constantly to re-evaluate information and draw their own conclusions. In so doing, Trifonov proved that even within the constricting boundaries of Socialist Realism, a talented writer can approach truthfulness and objectivity and stir the imagination of his readers.

NOTES

1. Natalia Ivanova, *Proza Iuriia Trifonova* (Moscow, 1984).

2. Tatiana Patera, *Obzor tvorchestva i analiz moskovskikh povestei Iuriia Trifonova* (Ann Arbor, 1983).

3. John Updike, "Czarist Shadows, Soviet Lilacs," *The New Yorker,* 11 September 1978, p. 153.

4. Richard Lourie, "Tales of a Soviet Chekhov," *The New York Times Book Review,* 18 March 1984, p. 7.

5. A detailed biography of Valentin Andreevich can be found in Iu. Trifonov's *Otblesk kostra,* first serialized in *Znamia,* nos. 2-3 (1965), and published in book form by Sovetskii pisatel' in 1966.

6. The elitist life in "the house on the embankment" depicted in the novel under the same title, corresponds closely to Trifonov's childhood in the government house on Serafimovich Street; see Iu. Trifonov, *Dom na naberezhnoi, Druzhba narodov,* no. 1 (1976), pp. 83-167.

7. More details about Trifonov's childhood and youth are provided in his semi-autobiographical novels, *Vremia i mesto: Roman v trinadtsati glavakh, Druzhba narodov,* nos. 9-10 (1981), pp. 72-148, 22-108; and *Ischeznovenie, Druzhba narodov,* no. 1 (1987), pp. 6-95.

8. Iu. Trifonov, "Prodolzhitel'nye uroki," in *Prodolzhitel'nye uroki* (Moscow, 1973); rpt. in *Izbrannye proizvedeniia* (Moscow, 1978), II, 504.

9. Iu. Trifonov, "Shirokii diapazon," *Moskovskii komsomolets,* 12 April 1947.

10. Iu. Trifonov, "V stepi," *Molodaia gvardiia: Al'manakh molodykh pisatelei* (Moscow, 1948), II, 150-79; "Znakomye mesta," *Molodoi kolkhoznik,* no. 4 (1948), pp. 12-15.

11. Iu. Trifonov, *Studenty, Novyi mir,* nos. 10-11 (1950), pp. 56-175, 49-182. For more information about the publication of the novel and Trifonov's relations with Alexander Tvardovsky, see Trifonov, "Zapiski soseda," in *Izbrannye proizvedeniia,* II, 511-40.

12. *Zalog uspekha* never appeared in print. For reviews see V. Zalesskii, "Zalog

uspekha," *Vecherniaia Moskva,* 2 December 1953, p. 4; T. Chebotarevskaia, "Sud'ba molodogo talanta," *Moskovskii komsomolets,* 23 December 1953; V. Sappak, "Zamysel obiazyvaet," *Teatr,* no 3 (1954), pp. 99-102.

13. A. Bocharov, "Voskhozhdenie," *Oktiabr',* no. 8 (1975), p. 204.

14. Iu. Trifonov, "Puti v pustyne," *Znamia,* no. 2 (1959), pp. 70-99; *Pod solntsem* (Moscow, 1959).

15. Iu. Trifonov, *V kontse sezona* (Moscow, 1961), *Kostry i dozhd'* (Moscow, 1965).

16. Iu. Trifonov, *Utolenie zhazhdy, Znamia,* nos. 4-7 (1963).

17. Trifonov did not receive the prize in 1965. He had to wait ten more years to be awarded a rather insignificant medal "The Badge of Honor"; see *Literaturnaia gazeta,* 3 September 1975, p. 3.

18. Iu. Trifonov, "Otblesk kostra," *Znamia,* nos. 2-3 (1965).

19. Iu. Trifonov, "Vera i Zoika," *Novyi mir,* no. 12 (1966), pp. 75-85; "Byl letnii polden'," *Novyi mir,* no. 12 (1966), pp. 85-91; "Samyi malen'kii gorod," *Novyi mir,* no. 1 (1968), pp. 74-80; "V gribnuiu osen'," *Novyi mir,* no. 8 (1968), pp. 67-75.

20. Iu. Trifonov, "Obmen," *Novyi mir,* no. 12 (1969), pp. 29-65; "Predvaritel'nye itogi," *Novyi mir,* no. 12 (1970), pp. 101-40; "Dolgoe proshchanie," *Novyi mir,* no. 8 (1971), pp. 53-107.

21. After his second twelve-year term as editor of *Novyi mir,* Alexander Tvardovsky was forced to resign in 1970; for more information see: D. Brown, *Soviet Russian Literature since Stalin* (London, 1978), pp. 74-79.

22. A. Bocharov, "Voskhozhdenie," p. 205.

23. Cf. A. Bocharov, ibid., pp. 203-11; V. Pertsovskii, "Ispytanie bytom," *Novyi mir,* no. 11 (1974), pp. 236-51; F. Kuznetsov, "Byt' chelovekom" *Oktiabr,* no. 8 (1975), pp. 193-203.

24. Cf. L. Fink, "Zybkost' kharaktera ili zybkost' zamysla," *Literaturnaia gazeta,* 29 October 1975, p. 4; N. Klado, "Prokrustovo lozhe byta," *Literaturnaia gazeta,* 12 July 1978, p. 4.

25. Iu. Trifonov, "Vybirat', reshat'sia, zhertvovat'," *Novyi mir,* no. 2 (1972), pp. 62-65.

26. Iu. Trifonov, "Vozvrashchenie k prosus," *Voprosy literatury,* no. 7 (1969), pp. 63-67.

27. Iu. Trifonov, "Neskonchaemoe nachalo," *Literaturnaia Rossiia,* 21 December 1973.

28. Iu. Trifonov, *Prodolzhitel'nye uroki* (Moscow, 1973).

29. Iu. Trifonov, *Neterpenie, Novyi mir,* nos. 3-5 (1973), pp. 44-116, 35-112, 8-90; rpt. in book form by Politizdat the same year.

30. Iu. Trifonov, *Drugaia zhizn', Novyi mir,* no. 8 (1975), pp. 7-99; *Dom na naberezhnoi, Druzhba narodov,* no. 1 (1976), pp. 83-167.

31. V. Tendriakov, "Zatmenie," *Druzhba narodov,* no. 5 (1977); F. Iskander, "Vozmezdie," *Druzhba narodov,* no. 3 (1977); E. Popov, "Rasskazy," *Druzhba narodov,* no. 3 (1977).

32. Iu. Trifonov, *Starik, Druzhba narodov,* no. 3 (1978), pp. 27-152; *Vremia i mesto: Roman v trinadtsati glavakh, Druzhba narodov,* no. 9-10 (1981), pp. 72-148, 22-108.

33. Iu. Trifonov, "Oprokinutyi dom," *Novyi mir,* no. 7 (1981), pp. 58-87.

34. Iu. Trifonov, "Knigi, kotorye vybiraiut nas," *Literaturnaia gazeta,* 10 November 1976, p. 6.

35. Iu. Trifonov, *Studenty, Novyi mir,* nos. 10-11 (1950), pp. 56-175, 49-182. In his memoirs "The Notes of a Neighbor," Trifonov acknowledges the help of Konstantin Fedin, his teacher at the Literary Institute, in recommending the novel for publication in *Novyi mir;* see "Zametki soseda," *Izbrannye proizvedeniia* (Moscow, 1978), II, 512-13.

36. G. Konovalov, *Universitet, Oktiabr'*, no. 6 (1947); V. Dobrovol'skii, *Troe v serykh shineliakh* (Moscow, 1947); *Zhenia Maslova* (Moscow, 1948); K. Lokotkov, *Vernost'* (Moscow, 1949).

37. It was a common tendency in Soviet literature to portray this type of "bourgeois" heroine. See X. Gasiorowska, *Women in Soviet Fiction* (Madison, 1968).

38. For more details on "conflictless" literature see: E. Brown, *Russian Literature since the Revolution* (New York, 1963); M. Slonim, *Soviet Russian Literature: Writers and Problems* (New York, 1964); G. Struve, *Russian Literature under Lenin and Stalin* (Norman, 1951).

39. A. Lozhechko, "Povest' o studentakh," *Oktiabr'*, no. 1 (1951), p. 187.

40. Ibid.

41. B. Galanov, "Nachalo puti," *Znamia*, no. 1 (1951), p. 173.

42. A. Lozhechko, p. 186.

43. S. L'vov, "Povest' o sovetskikh studentakh," in *Vydaiushchiesia proizvedeniia sovetskoi literatury 1950 goda: Sbornik statei* (Moscow, 1952), pp. 267-68.

44. B. Galanov, p. 173.

45. A. Lozhechko, p. 188.

46. Iu. Trifonov, "Roman s istoriei," *Voprosy literatury*, no. 5 (1982), p. 71.

47. Iu. Trifonov, "Doktor, student i Mitia," *Molodaia gvardiia*, no. 2 (1956); "Posledniaia okhota," *Literaturnaia gazeta*, 15 September 1956; "Konets sezona," *Ogonek*, no. 32 (1956).

48. Iu. Trifonov, "Neskonchaemoe nachalo," *Literaturnaia Rossiia*, 21 December 1973; rpt. in *Izbrannye proizvedeniia* (Moscow, 1978), II, 495.

49. Iu. Trifonov, "Puti v pustyne," *Znamia*, no. 2 (1959), pp. 70-98; rpt. as *Pod solntsem* (Moscow, 1959).

50. V. Shklovskii, "Iskusstvo kak priem," *Poetika: Sborniki po teorii poeticheskogo iazyka* (Petrograd, 1919).

51. L. Lazarev, "Bez egzotiki," *Druzhba narodov*, no. 6 (1959), p. 228.

52. Iu. Trifonov, "Stariki v Kaushute," *Pod solntsem;* rpt. in *Izbrannye proizvedeniia*, I, 117.

53. L. Lazarev, p. 227.

54. Z. Finitskaia, "Pod iarkim solntsem," *Oktiabr'*, no. 12 (1960), p. 213.

55. Iu. Trifonov, *V kontse sezona* (Moscow, 1961).

56. Iu. Trifonov, "Prozrachnoe solntse oseni," *Fizkul'tura i sport*, no. 7 (1959); rpt. in *V kontse sezona*.

57. Iu. Trifonov, "Konets sezona," *Ogonek*, no. 32 (1956); rpt. in *V kontse sezona*.

58. Iu. Trifonov, "Pobeditel' shvedov," *Sovetskii sport*, 29-30 March 1958; rpt. in *V kontse sezona*.

59. Iu. Trifonov, "Stimul," *Fizkul'tura i sport*, no. 6 (1958); rpt in *V kontse sezona*.

60. Iu. Trifonov, "Daleko v gorakh," *Fizkul'tura i sport*, no. 11 (1957); rpt. in *V kontse sezona*.

61. Iu. Trifonov, *Fakely nad Flaminio* (Moscow, 1965); *Kepka s bol'shim kozyr'kom* (Moscow, 1969); *Igry v sumerkakh* (Moscow, 1970).

62. The long delay in publishing *The Quenching of Thirst* was caused by the shutdown in the construction of the Kara-Kum canal in the mid-fifties, which forced Trifonov to abandon the novel. When the construction re-opened in 1958, Trifonov promptly finished the novel and submitted it for publication to *Znamia*, no. 4-7 (1963); it was published in book form by Khudozhestvennaia literatura in 1963.

63. M. Shaginian, *Gidrotsentral'* (Moscow, 1931); F. Gladkov, *Energiia, Novyi mir,* nos. 7-10 (1932); V. Kataev, *Vremia, vpered!* (Moscow, 1932); I. Erenburg, *Den' vtoroi*

(Moscow, 1932).

64. For more details on the early industrial novel see: S. Shput, *Tema sotsialisticheskogo stroitel'stva v proze 20-ykh godov* (Moscow, 1963); L. Ershov, *Russkii sovetskii roman: Natsional'nye traditsii i novatorstvo* (Moscow, 1967); H. Borland, *Soviet Literary Theory and Practice During the First Five-Year Plan* (New York, 1950).

65. B. Ettinhof, "Art in the Five-Year Plan," *VOKS Bulletin*, no. 10-12 (1931), p. 4.

66. V. Azhaev, *Daleko ot Moskvy* (Moscow, 1948); V. Gorbatov, *Donbas* (Moscow, 1950); V. Kochetov, *Zhurbiny* (Moscow, 1952).

67. L. Terekopian, "Poznanie kharaktera," *Druzhba narodov*, no. 12 (1969), pp. 234-46. Terekopian's views are shared by other Soviet critics, see: L. Anninskii, "Real'nost' prozy," *Don*, no. 3 (1964), pp. 152-58; F. Kuznetsov, "Nastuplenie novoi nravstvennosti," *Voprosy literatury*, no. 2 (1964), pp. 3-26; V. Savataev, "Molodost' dushi," *Nash sovremennik*, no. 7 (1973), pp. 167-73.

68. G. Vladimov, *Bol'shaia ruda*, *Novyi mir*, no. 7 (1961); V. Kozhevnikov, *Znakomtes', Baluev* (Moscow, 1960); V. Lipatov, *Skazanie o direktore Pronchatove* (Moscow, 1969).

69. A. Bocharov, "Kanal eto v sushchnosti zhizn'," *Druzhba narodov*, no. 12 (1963), p. 268.

70. The theme of moral renewal appeared in many works, written in the late 1950s and 1960s, cf. V. Dudintsev, *Ne khlebom edinym* (Moscow, 1956); V. Nekrasov, *Kira Georgievna* (Moscow, 1961); D. Granin, *Idu na grozu* (Moscow, 1962); I. Dombrovskii, *Khranitel' vechnosti* (Moscow, 1964).

71. A. Bocharov, "Kanal eto v sushchnosti zhizn'," p. 267.

72. F. Kuznetsov, "Nastuplenie novoi nravstvennosti," p. 7.

73. F. Svetov, "Utolenie zhazhdy," *Novyi mir*, no. 11 (1963), p. 239.

74. I. Tikhonov, "Delo, kotoromu ty sluzhish'," *Oktiabr'*, no. 1 (1964), p. 214.

75. A. Turkov, "Byt, chelovek, istoriia," in Iu. Trifonov, *Izbrannye proizvedeniia* (Moscow, 1978), I, 9.

76. Cf. Trifonov's remarks in his interview "Roman s istoriei," *Voprosy literatury*, no. 5 (1982), p. 71.

77. Iu. Trifonov, "Vera i Zoika," "Byl letnii polden'," *Novyi mir*, no. 12 (1966), pp. 75-91; "Samyi malen'kii gorod," *Novyi mir*, no. 1 (1968), pp. 74-80; "V gribnuiu osen'," *Novyi mir*, no. 8 (1968), pp. 67-75.

78. Iu. Trifonov, "Puteshestvie," rpt. in *Izbrannye proizvedeniia* (Moscow, 1978), I, 23-26.

79. Trifonov's preoccupation with everyday life was acknowledged by all the reviewers of *Kepka s bol'shim kozyrkom* and *Rasskazy i povesti;* cf. E. Babaev, "Rasskazy romanista," *Novyi mir*, no. 9 (1970), pp. 268-72; T. Nikol'skaia, Review of *Rasskazy i povesti, Zvezda*, no. 2 (1972), pp. 215-16; I. Shtokman, "Volny moria zhiteiskogo," *Iunost'*, no. 6 (1972), pp. 62-65.

80. Iu. Trifonov, "Vybirat', reshat'sia, zhertvovat'," *Novyi mir*, no. 2 (1972), p. 70.

81. Iu. Trifonov, "Vera i Zoika," rpt. in *Izbrannye proizvedeniia*, I, 149.

82. Iu. Trifonov, "Byl letnii polden'," rpt. in *Izbrannye proizvedeniia*, I, 165.

83. Iu. Trifonov, "V gribnuiu osen'," rpt. in *Izbrannye proizvedeniia*, I, 199-211.

84. A. Bocharov, "Voskhozhdenie," *Oktiabr'*, no. 8 (1975), pp. 203-11.

85. Iu. Trifonov, "Taking Stock," *The Long Goodbye* (Ann Arbor, 1978), p. 111. This edition will be used hereafter.

86. For a more detailed analysis of the thematic and ideological aspects of the Moscow novellas see: E. Alekserova, "Moskovskie povesti I. Trifonova," *Uchenye zapiski Azerbaidzhanskogo pedagogicheskogo instituta*, 3 (Baku, 1976), 50-53; O. Talanova, "Khudozhestvennaia manera Iu. Trifonova," in *Problemy poetiki* (Alma-Ata, 1980), pp.

101-12; N. Ivanova, *Proza Iuriia Trifonova* (Moscow, 1984), pp. 98-211; N. Shneidman, "Iurii Trifonov and the Ethics of Contemporary City Life," *Canadian Slavonic Papers*, XIX, 3 (1977), 335-51; A. Hughes, "Bol'shoi mir ili zamknutyi mirok: Departure from Literary Convention in Iu. Trifonov's Recent Fiction," *Canadian Slavonic Papers*, XXII, 4 (1980), 470-80; C. Maegd-Soep, "The Theme of Byt in the Stories of Iu. Trifonov," *Russian Literature and Criticism: Selected Papers from the Second World Congress* (Berkeley, 1982), pp. 49-62.

87. Iu. Trifonov, "The Exchange," *The Long Goodbye*, p. 20.

88. The term "concealed narrator" is taken from an article by C. Gordon and A. Tate, "Notes of Fictional Technique," published in *The House of Fiction* (New York, 1960), pp. 435-58. See also W. C. Booth, *Rhetoric of Fiction* (Chicago, 1961); N. Friedman, "Point of View in Fiction: The Development of a Critical Concept," *Publications of the Modern Language Association of America* (1955), 1160-84.

89. Cf. an interesting study of the novella's structure by L. I. Levina, "Siuzhetno-kompozitsionnye sredstva vyrazheniia soderzhaniia v povesti Iu. Trifonova 'Obmen'," *Sbornik nauchnykh trudov Tashkentskogo universiteta*, 578 (Tashkent, 1978), 40-55.

90. Iu. Trifonov, "Taking Stock," *The Long Goodbye*, p. 101.

91. Cf. T. Rybal'chenko, "Zhanrovaia struktura i khudozhestvennaia ideia: Povest' Iu. Trifonova 'Predvaritel'nye itogi'," *Problemy metoda i zhanra* (Tomsk, 1977), pp. 98-105.

92. Iu. Trifonov, "The Long Goodbye," *The Long Goodbye*, p. 203.

93. Iu. Trifonov, "Another Life," *Another Life. The House on the Embankment* (New York, 1983), p. 11. This edition will be used hereafter.

94. Cf. two revealing studies on Trifonov's use of interior monologue: G. A. Belaia, "O vnutrennei i vneshnei teme: Povest' Iu. Trifonova 'Drugaia zhizn'," *Nauchnye doklady vysshikh shkol: Filologicheskie nauki*, 2 (1983), 10-17; O. A. Kutmina, "Vnutrennii monolog v povesti Iu. Trifonova 'Drugaia zhizn': Nekotorye aspekty," *Problemy psikhologizma v khudozhestvennoi literature: Sbornik statei* (Tomsk, 1980), pp. 44-49.

95. G. Brovman, "Izmereniia malogo mira," *Literaturnaia gazeta*, 8 March 1972, p. 5.

96. L. Fink, "Zybkost' kharaktera ili zybkost' zamysla," *Literaturnaia gazeta*, 29 October 1975, p. 4.

97. V. Bednenko, O. Krinitskii, "Prezhdevremennye itogi," *Molodaia gvardiia*, no. 10 (1971), pp. 305-9.

98. M. Gus, "Zhizn' i sushchestvovanie," *Znamia*, no. 8 (1972), pp. 211-26.

99. V. Dudintsev, "Stoit li umirat' ran'she vremeni?" *Literaturnoe obozrenie*, no. 4 (1976), pp. 52-57.

100. V. Bednenko, p. 308.

101. L. Andreev, "Sovremennik: Delo i slovo," *Literaturnaia gazeta*, 12 July 1978, p. 4.

102. L. Anninskii, "Neokonchatel'nye itogi," *Don*, no. 5 (1972), pp. 183-92.

103. I. Sozonova, "Vnutri kruga," *Literaturnoe obozrenie*, no. 5 (1976), pp. 53-56.

104. I. Grinberg, "Perekrestki i paralleli," *Oktiabr'*, no. 12 (1974), pp. 189-204.

105. B. Bazhenov, "Kakoi ei byt' zhizni?" *Oktiabr'*, no. 12 (1975), pp. 210-12.

106. M. Amusin, "Voprosy, poiski, obreteniia," *Zvezda*, no. 11 (1982), pp. 182-91.

107. V. Pertsovskii, "Ispytanie bytom," *Novyi mir*, no. 11 (1974), pp. 236-51.

108. N. Tiulpinov, "Otblesk drugoi zhizni," *Zvezda*, no. 2 (1976), pp. 216-18.

109. A. Bocharov, "Voskhozhdenie," *Oktiabr'*, no. 8 (1975), pp. 203-11.

110. Ibid.

111. L. Anninskii, "Neokonchatel'nye itogi," p. 183; A. Turkov, "Byt, chelovek, istoriia," in Iu. Trifonov, *Izbrannye proizvedeniia*, I, pp. 8-9.

112. Vladimir Tendryakov, "Apostol'skaia komandirovka," *Novyi mir,* nos. 8-10 (1969); "Noch' posle vypuska," *Novyi mir,* no. 9 (1974); "Zatmenie," *Druzhba narodov,* no. 5 (1977); "Rasplata," *Novyi mir,* no. 3 (1979).

113. Daniil Granin, *Iskateli, Zvezda,* nos. 7-8 (1954); "Sobstvennoe mnenie," *Novyi mir,* no. 8 (1956); Idu na grozu (Moscow, 1962); "Dozhd' v chuzhom gorode," *Neva,* no. 1 (1973); "Odnofamilets," *Zvezda,* no. 3 (1975).

114. I. Grekova, "Za prokhodnoi," *Novyi mir,* no. 6 (1962); "Na ispytaniiakh," *Novyi mir,* no. 7 (1967); "Khoziaika gostinitsy," *Zvezda,* no. 9 (1976); "Kafedra," *Novyi mir,* no. 9 (1978).

115. Cf. the definition of the novel in M. H. Abrams, *A Glossary of Literary Terms* (New York, 1957), p. 110. Although the majority of critics agree that *The House on the Embankment* displays many novelistic features, they still prefer to classify it as a novella; see N. Leiderman, "Potentsial zhanra," *Sever,* no. 3 (1978), pp. 105-9; N. Ivanova, *Proza Iuriia Trifonova* (Moscow, 1984), pp. 212-59.

116. Iu. Trifonov, "The House on the Embankment," in *Another Life. The House on the Embankment* (New York, 1983), pp. 187-350. This edition will be used hereafter.

117. In her study *Obzor tvorchestva i analiz moskovskikh povestei Iuriia Trifonova* (Ann Arbor, 1983), Tatiana Patera considers the voice of the second narrator to be the voice of the author. Despite biographical and personal similarities between the two, they should not be so identified, for they perform different functions. Whereas the voice of the author usually assumes omniscience and authority, the voice of the second narrator is restricted to reporting only facts he has witnessed, and offers subjective opinions.

118. It is hard to agree with Tatiana Patera that the epilogue scene takes place in 1971, i.e., before the meeting between Glebov and Lev. Placed at the very end of the novel, and outlining the subsequent fate of Lev, the narrator and Professor Ganchuk, it has all the features of an epilogue, and as such should be dated as 1974. Cf. T. Patera, *Obzor tvorchestva,* pp. 306-7.

119. Many Soviet reviewers criticized *The House on the Embankment* for its inadequate portrayal of Soviet life and the separation of the protagonists from social and political interests; cf. N. Klado, "Prokrustovo lozhe byta," *Literaturnaia gazeta,* 12 May 1976, p. 4; B. Pankin, "Po krugu ili po spirali," *Druzhba narodov,* no. 5 (1977), pp. 328-53; V. Pertsovskii, "Pokoriaias' techeniiu," *Voprosy literatury,* no. 4 (1979), pp. 3-35.

120. For a detailed analysis of the novel's political connotations see S. McLaughlin, "Jurij Trifonov's *House on the Embankment:* Narration and Meaning," *Slavic and East European Journal,* XXVI, 4 (1982), 419-33; T. Patera, *Obzor tvorchestva,* pp. 256-318.

121. For a more detailed analysis of the affinities between *Students* and *The House on the Embankment,* see V. Kozhinov, "Problema avtora i put' pisatelia," *Kontekst: Literaturno-kriticheskie issledovaniia* (1977), pp. 22-47.

122. B. Bondarenko, *Piramida* (Moscow, 1976); A. Kron, *Bessonnitsa, Novyi mir,* nos. 4-6 (1977); I. Grekova, *Kafedra, Novyi mir,* no. 9 (1978); V. Kaverin, *Dvukhchasovaia progulka, Novyi mir,* no. 11 (1978).

123. For a detailed discussion of Soviet literature on science see: R. J. Marsh, *Soviet Fiction Since Stalin: Science, Politics and Literature* (London, 1986).

124. Iu. Trifonov, *Neterpenie, Novyi mir,* nos. 3-5 (1973), pp. 44-116, 35-112, 8-90; rpt. in book form as *Neterpenie* (Moscow, 1973).

125. M. Popovskii, *Pobezhdennoe vremia* (Moscow, 1975); V. Voinovich, *Stepen' doveriia* (Moscow, 1972); I. Davydov, *Mart* (Moscow, 1966); *Glukhaia pora listopada* (Moscow, 1970); *Zaveshchaiu vam brat'ia* (Moscow, 1975).

For more information on the above novels, see V. Oskotskii, "Roman i istoriia," *Voprosy literatury,* no. 8 (1973), pp. 3-45; M. Perelygina, "Osobennosti zhanra i siuzhetno-kompozitsionnoi struktury sovremennoi istoriko-biograficheskoi povesti o narodovol'tsakh," *Nauchnye trudy Kuibyshevskogo pedagogicheskogo instituta,* 227 (Kuibyshev, 1979), 80-94.

126. V. Dolgii, *Porog* (Moscow, 1974).

127. Iu. Trifonov, *Neterpenie,* rpt. in *Izbrannye proizvedeniia* (Moscow, 1978), I, 631. This edition will be used hereafter.

128. For a detailed discussion of this aspect of *Neterpenie,* see F. Kuznetsov, "Dukhovnye tsennosti," *Novyi mir,* no. 1 (1974), pp. 211-31; S. Shtut, "Rassuzhdeniia i opisaniia," *Voprosy literatury,* no. 10 (1975), pp. 38-72. A. Lebedev, "Neterpimost'," in *Vybor* (Moscow, 1980), pp. 193-246.

129. Only a few Soviet studies deal with the question of the novel's structure; see N. Il'ina, "Iz rodoslovnoi russkoi revolutsii," *Neman,* no. 12 (1978), pp. 170-75; M. Perelygina, "Osobennosti zhanra," pp. 80-94.

130. N. Naumova, "Sviaz' vremen," *Zvezda,* no. 6 (1976), pp. 195-202.

131. V. Oskotskii, "Nravstvennye uroki Narodnoi Voli," *Literaturnoe obozrenie,* no. 11 (1973), pp. 55-60; V. Kardin, "Proroki v svoem otechestve," *Druzhba narodov,* no. 8 (1974), pp. 267-76.

132. A. Filatova, "Postigaia istoriiu," pp. 169-77.

133. M. Perelygina, "Osobennosti zhanra," pp. 80-94.

134. Iu. Trifonov, "Voobrazit' beskonechnost'," *Literaturnoe obozrenie,* no. 4 (1977), pp. 98-102.

135. Iu. Trifonov, *Starik, Druzhba narodov,* no. 3 (1978), pp. 27-152. The novel was published in book form as *Starik. Drugaia zhizn'* (Moscow: Sovetskii pisatel', 1980). The latter edition will be used hereafter.

136. Trifonov's interest in the historical past as a means to reveal the present is discussed in A. Bocharov, "Strast' bor'by i igrushechnye strasti," *Literaturnoe obozrenie,* no. 10 (1978), pp. 64-67; N. Paleeva, "Sviaz' vremen," *Molodaia gvardiia,* no. 9 (1979), pp. 281-91; A. Pankov, "Zaboty zhizni i puti literatury," *Druzhba narodov,* no. 10 (1985), pp. 217-29.

137. Trifonov pointed out that he incorporated some authentic documents about F. K. Mironov, a historic Cossack commander who served as a prototype for the image of Migulin; see Iu. Trifonov, "Gorod i gorozhane," *Literaturnaia gazeta,* 28 March 1981, pp. 4-5. For more information on that question see: G. Ermolaev "Proshloe i nastoiashchee v 'Starike' Iu. Trifonova," *Russian Language Journal,* XXXVIII, 128 (1983), 131-46.

138. Uncle Shura in many ways resembles Trifonov's father and uncle, professional revolutionaries who dedicated their lives to the Revolution. Their fates are depicted in Iu. Trifonov, *Otblesk kostra* (Moscow, 1966).

139. The conflict between the three generations of the Letunov family is discussed in I. Velembovskaia, "Simpatii i antipatii Iuriia Trifonova," *Novyi mir,* no. 9 (1980), pp. 255-58.

140. V. M. Sinelnikov, "Poznat' cheloveka, poznat' vremia," *Voprosy literatury,* no. 9 (1979), p. 51.

141. V. Khmara, "Protivostoianie," *Literaturnaia gazeta,* 28 June 1978, p. 5.

142. Iu. Trifonov, "Oprokinutyi dom," *Novyi mir,* no. 7 (1981), pp. 58-87. This edition will be used hereafter.

143. Cf. Iu. Trifonov, "Vospominanie o Dzhentsano," *Molodaia gvardiia,* no. 4 (1964).

144. Cf. the remarks on the importance of the theme of death and dying for Trifonov's works in Norman Shneidman's "The New Dimensions of Time and Place in Yury Trifonov's Prose of the 1980s," *Canadian Slavonic Papers,* XXVII, 2 (1985), 188-95.

145. Cf. Iu. Trifonov, "Puti v pustyne," *Znamia,* no. 2 (1959), pp. 70-98.

146. V. Amlinskii, "O dniakh edinstvennykh," *Literaturnoe obozrenie,* no. 1 (1982), pp. 42-45.

147. M. Zolotonosov, "Sviaz' vremen," *Neva*, no. 6 (1982), pp. 152-53.

148. Iu. Trifonov, "Another Life" in *The House on the Embankment. Another Life* (New York: 1983), p. 111.

149. Iu. Trifonov, *Vremia i mesto: Roman v trinadtsati glavakh, Druzhba narodov*, nos. 9-10 (1981), pp. 72-148, 22-108. This edition will be used hereafter.

150. Rulf Schroeder, "Gespraeche mit Juri Trifonov," *Weimarer Beitrage*, no. 8 (1981). The interview was later reprinted in Russian as "Roman s istoriei," *Voprosy literatury*, no. 5 (1982), pp. 66-77.

151. "Punktir" literally means a dotted line, but it is also used to describe an impressionistic technique of applying dots or tiny strokes to a surface, so that when seen from a distance the dots or strokes blend luminously together. It is the latter meaning of the word that Trifonov had in mind when he described his novel as "punktir." Ibid., p. 76.

152. A Bocharov, "Listopad," *Literaturnoe obozrenie*, no. 3 (1982), p. 45.

153. Actually, at one point in the novel, the author-narrator is referred to as Andryusha, but the reader never learns his patronymic or last name; see *Vremia i mesto*, p. 111.

154. Cf. the analysis of the novel's structure in V. Golovskoi, "Nravstvennye uroki trifonovskoi prozy," *Russian Language Journal*, XXXVII, 128 (1983), pp. 147-64.

155. For more information on the similarity between Trifonov and the author-narrator, as well as Antipov, see A. Bocharov, "Listopad," p. 46.

156. See the excellent analysis of this question in S. Eremina and V. Piskunov, "Vremia i mesto prozy Iuriia Trifonova," *Voprosy literatury*, no. 5 (1982), pp. 58-64.

157.Trifonov's treatment of the theme of creative writing is discussed in V. Boborykin, "Khleb khudozhnika," *Literaturnaia Rossiia*, 9 April 1982, p. 8; E. Stepanenko, "Tainstvo tvorchestva," *Sever*, no. 2 (1985), pp. 110-16.

158. S. Eremina, V. Piskunov, p. 64.

159. Iu. Trifonov, *Ischeznovenie, Druzhba narodov*, no. 1 (1987), pp. 6-95. This edition will be used hereafter.

160. V. Kardin, "Vremena ne vybiraiut: Iz zapisok o Iu. Trifonove," *Novyi mir*, no. 7 (1987), p. 239.

161. This quality of the novel was stressed by most of the reviewers, cf. Obozrevatel', "Chuvstvo puti," *Literaturnaia Rossiia*, 13 February 1987, p. 5; A. Latynina, "Oskolok gologramy," *Literaturnaia gazeta*, 18 February 1987, p. 7; A. Turkov, "Ne boias' povtorit'sia," *Znamia*, no. 5 (1987), pp. 232-34.

162. Cf. C. Gordon, A. Tate, "Notes on Fictional Techniques," pp. 442-43.

163. A. Latynina, p. 7

164. V. Shklovskii, "Iskusstvo kak priem," *Poetika: Sborniki po teorii poeticheskogo iazyka* (Petrograd, 1919), pp. 101-14.

165. I. Gladil'shchikov, "Ne ischeznovenie: Pamiat'," *Literaturnaia Rossiia*, 27 March 1987, p. 2.

166. A. Rybakov's *Deti Arbata* was completed in 1965 and announced for publication by *Novyi mir*, no. 12 (1966) and by *Oktiabr'*, no. 9 (1978), but failed to appear. It was published in *Druzhba narodov*, nos. 4-6 (1987).

167. A. Bek's *Novoe naznachenie* was written in 1964 and had to wait more than twenty years for publication. It appeared in *Znamia*, nos. 10-11 (1986).

168. V. Amlinskii, *Opravdan budet kazhdyi chas: Povest' ob ottse, Iunost'*, nos. 10-11 (1986).

SELECTED BIBLIOGRAPHY

PRIMARY SOURCES

"V stepi." *Molodaia gvardiia: Al'manakh molodykh pisatelei*. Moskva: Molodaia gvardiia, 1948, II, 150-79.

"Znakomye mesta." *Molodoi kolkhoznik*, no. 4 (1948), pp. 12-15.

Studeny. Novyi mir, nos. 10-11 (1950), pp 56-175, 49-182.

Studeny. Moskva: Molodaia gvardiia, 1951.

"Doktor, student i Mitia." *Molodaia gvardiia*, no. 1 (1956).

"Sluchainyi sosed." *Ogonek*, no. 32 (1956).

"Posledniaia okhota." *Literaturnaia gazeta*, 15 September 1956.

"Neokonchennyi kholst." *Neva*, no. 3 (1957), pp. 87-94.

"Pobeditel' shvedov." *Sovetskii sport*, 29-30 March 1958.

"Stimul." *Fizkul'tura i sport*, no. 6 (1958).

"Puti v pustyne." *Znamia*, no. 2 (1959), pp. 70-99.

"Prozrachnoe solntse oseni." *Fizkul'tura i sport*, no. 7 (1959).

Pod solntsem: Rasskazy. Moskva: Sovetskii pisatel', 1959.

"Odnazhdy dushnoi noch'iu." *Tarusskie stranitsy*. Kaluga: Kaluzhskoe knizhnoe izdatel'stvo, 1961.

Utolenie zhazhdy. Znamia, nos. 4-7 (1963).

Utolenie zhazhdy. Moskva: Khudozhestvennaia literatura, 1963.

Kostry i dozhd': Rasskazy. Moskva: Sovetskaia Rossiia, 1964.

Fakely nad Flaminio: Rasskazy, ocherki, razmyshleniia i kartiny, nabroski perom i vospominaniia o puteshestviiakh po stranam i stadionam. Moskva: Fizkul'tura i sport, 1965.

Otblesk kostra. Znamia, nos. 2-3 (1965).

Otblesk kostra. Moskva: Sovetskii pisatel', 1966.

"Vera i Zoika," "Byl letnii polden'." *Novyi mir*, no. 12 (1966), pp. 75-91.

"Pobeditel'." *Znamia*, no. 7 (1968).

"Samyi malen'kii gorod." *Novyi mir*, no. 1 (1968), pp. 74-80.
"V gribnuiu osen'." *Novyi mir*, no. 8 (1968), pp. 67-75.
Kepka s bol'shim kozyr'kom. Moskva: Sovetskaia Rossiia, 1969.
"Obmen." *Novyi mir*,,no. 12 (1969), pp. 29-65.
Igry v sumerkakh. Moskva: Fizkul'tura i sport, 1970.
"Beskonechnye igry." *Prostor*, no. 7 (1970).
"Predvaritel'nye itogi." *Novyi mir*, no. 12 (1970), pp. 101-140.
Rasskazy i povesti. Moskva: Khudozhestvennaia literatura, 1971.
"Dolgoe proshchanie." *Novyi mir*, no. 8 (1971), pp. 53-107.
Dolgoe proshchanie: Povesti i rasskazy. Moskva: Sovetskaia Rossiia, 1973.
Neterpenie. *Novyi mir*, nos. 3-5 (1973), pp. 44-116, 35-112, 8-90.
Neterpenie. Moskva: Politizdat, 1973.
"The Exchange." *The Ardis Anthology of Recent Russian Literature*. Ed. by Carl Proffer and Ellendea Proffer. Ann Arbor: Ardis, 1973, pp. 117-164.
Prodolzhitel'nye uroki. Moskva: Sovetskaia Rossiia, 1975.
"Drugaia zhizn'." *Novyi mir*, no. 8 (1975), pp. 7-99.
Drugaia zhizn'. Moskva: Sovetskaia Rossia, 1976.
Dom na naberezhnoi. *Druzhba narodov*, no. 1 (1976), pp. 83-167.
Izbrannye proizvedeniia v dvukh tomakh. Moskva: Khudozhestvennaia literatura, 1978
Povesti. Moskva: Sovetskaia Rossiia, 1978.
Starik. Drugaia zhizn', Moskva: Sovetskii pisatel', 1979.
"Oprokinutyi dom." *Novyi mir*, no. 7 (1981), pp. 58-87.
Vremia i mesto: Roman v trinadtsati glavakh. *Druzhba narodov*, nos. 9-10 (1981), pp. 72-148, 22-108.
Another Life. The House on the Embankment. Tr. by Michael Glenny. New York: Simon and Schuster, 1983.
Vechnye temy. Moskva: Sovetskii pisatel', 1984.
The Old Man. Tr. by Jacqueline Edwards. New York: Simon and Schuster, 1984.
Sobranie sochinenii v chetyrekh tomakh. Moskva: Khudozhestvennaia literatura, 1985.
Ischeznovenie. *Druzhba narodov*, no. 1 (1987), pp. 6-95.
Moskovskie povesti. Moskva: Sovetskaia Rossiia, 1988.
Otblesk kostra. Ischeznovenie. Moskva: Sovetskii pisatel', 1988.

SECONDARY SOURCES

Akmuradova, A. "Nekotorye khudozhestvennye osobennosti romana I. Trifonova 'Utolenie zhazhdy'." *Izvestiia Akademii nauk Turkmenskoi SSR*, no. 5 (1975), pp. 64-70.
Aleksandrov, M. "Sport i zhizn'." *Znamia*, no. 10 (1970), pp. 248-50.
Alekserova, E. A. "Turkmenskie rasskazy 50-ykh godov i ikh rol' v tvorchestve I. V. Trifonova." *Uchenye zapiski Azerbaidzhanskogo pedagogicheskogo instituta*, no. 2 (1975), pp. 141-45.
_____. "Roman 'Utolenie zhazhdy': Opyt osvoeniia zhizni." *Uchenye zapiski Azerbaidzhanskogo pedagogicheskogo instituta*, no. 5 (1975), pp. 113-19.
_____. "Moskovskie povesti I. Trifonova." *Uchenye zapiski Azerbaidzhanskogo pedagogicheskogo instituta*, no. 3 (1976), pp. 50-53.
_____. "Stanovlenie nravstvennoi problematiki v tvorchestve I. Trifonova." Diss. Tbiliskii gosudarstvennyi universitet. Tbilisi, 1978.
Amlinskii, V. "O dniakh edinstvennykh." *Literaturnoe obozrenie*, no.1 (1982), pp. 42-45.
Amusin, M. "Voprosy, poiski, obreteniia." *Zvezda*, no. 11 (1982), pp. 182-91.
Andreev, I. "V zamknutom mirke." *Literaturnaia gazeta*, 3 March 1971, p. 5.

_____. "Sovremennik: delo i slovo." *Literaturnaia gazeta*, 12 June 1978, p. 4.

Anninskii, L. "Realnost' prozy." *Don*, no. 3 (1964), pp. 152-58.

_____. "Neokonchatel'nye itogi: O trekh povestiakh I. Trifonova." *Don*, no 5 (1972), pp. 183-92.

_____. "Ochishchenie proshlym: O povestiakh I. Trifonova'Drugaia zhizn' i 'Dom na naberezhnoi'." *Don*, no. 2 (1977), pp. 157-160.

_____. "Intelligenty i prochie." *Tridtsatye-semidesiatye: Literaturno—kriticheskie stat'i.* Moskva: 1977, pp. 197-227.

_____. "Rassechenie kornia: Zametki o publitsistike Iuriia Trifonova." *Druzhba narodov*, no. 2 (1985), pp. 239-46.

Austin, P. "From Helsingfors to Helsinki: Jurij Trifonov's Search for His Past." *Scando-Slavica*, 32 (1986), pp. 5-16.

Avtamonova, N. "Kogo vybiraet vremia?" *Sem'ia i shkola*, no. 7 (1988), pp. 48-50.

Babaev, E. "Rasskazy romanista." *Novyi mir*, no. 9 (1970), pp. 268-72.

Baranov, V. "Zhiznennye korni." *Novyi mir*, no. 8 (1977), pp. 240-49.

Baruzdin, S. "Neodnoznachnyi Trifonov." *Druzhba narodov*, no. 10 (1987), pp. 255-62.

Bazhenov, G. "Kakoi ei byt' zhizni!" *Oktiabr'*, no. 12 (1975), pp. 210-12.

Bednenko, V., Krinitskii, O. "Prezhdevremennye itogi." *Molodaia gvardiia*, no. 10 (1971), pp. 305-9.

Beitz, W. "Alltäglichkeit und Geschichte: Die Prosa Jurij Trifonovs." *Was kann denn ein Dichter auf Erden: Betrachtungen über moderne sowjetische Schriftsteller.* Eds. A. Hiersche, E. Kowalski. Berlin: Aufbau, 1982, pp. 428-54.

Belaia, G. "Nepovtorimoe odnazhdy: Filosofsko-eticheskaia tema v proze I. Trifonova." *Literaturnoe obozrenie*, no. 5 (1983), pp. 7-12.

_____. "O vnutrennei i vneshnei teme: Povest' I. Trifonova 'Drugaia zhizn'." *Nauchnye doklady vysshikh shkol: Filologicheskie nauki*, no. 2 (1983), pp. 10-17.

Boborykin, V. "Khleb khudozhnika." *Literaturnaia Rossiia*, 9 April 1982, p. 8.

Bocharov, A. "Kanal eto v sushchnosti zhizn'." *Druzhba narodov*, no. 12 (1963), pp. 267-70.

_____. "Vremia v chetyrekh izmereniiakh." *Voprosy literatury*, no. 11 (1974), pp. 33-68.

_____. "Ispytanie zhizn'iu." *Druzhba narodov*, no. 7 (1975), pp. 220-33.

_____. "Voskhozhdenie." *Oktiabr'*, no. 8 (1975), pp. 203-11.

_____. "Vremia kristallizatsii." *Voprosy literatury*, no. 3 (1976), pp. 29-75.

_____. "Strast' liubvi i igrushechnye strasti." *Literaturnoe obozrenie*, no. 10 (1978), pp. 64-67.

_____. "Kontrapunkt: Obshchee i individual'noe v tvorchestve I. Trifonova, V. Shukshina, V. Rasputina." *Oktiabr'*, no. 7 (1982), pp. 190-99.

_____. "Listopad." *Literaturnoe obozrenie*, no. 3 (1982), pp. 45-48.

Brovman, G. "Pravda istoricheskogo optimizma." *Moskva*, no. 1 (1964), pp. 186-95.

_____. "Zhivaia zhizn' i normativnost'." *Moskva*, no. 7 (1964), pp. 192-99.

_____. "Izmereniia malogo mira." *Literaturnaia gazeta*, 8 March 1972, p. 5.

Chapple, R. L., "Yury Trifonov and the Maturation of Soviet Literature." *Midwest Quarterly*, 29, 1 (1987), pp. 40-54.

Dedkov, I. "Vertikali Iuriia Trifonova." *Novyi mir*, no. 8 (1985), pp. 220-35.

Demidov, A. "Pokuda serdtse b'etsia." *Teatr*, no. 9 (1976), pp. 38-46.

_____. "Minuvshee." *Teatr*, no. 7 (1981), pp. 97-107.

Dudinstsev, V. "Stoit li umirat' ran'she vremeni?" *Literaturnoe obozrenie*, no. 4 (1976), pp. 52-57.

_____. "Velikii smysl zhit'." *Literaturnoe obozrenie*, no. 5 (1976), pp. 48-56.

Durkin, A. "Trifonov's 'Taking Stock': The Role of Cexovian Subtext." *Slavic and East*

European Journal, 28, no. 1 (1984), 32-41.

Dymshits, A. "Vospityvat' v cheloveke cheloveka." *Literaturnaia Rossiia,* 19 February 1965, pp. 6-7.

Eberstadt, F. "Out of the Drawer and into the West." *Commentary,* no. 1 (1985), pp. 36-44.

Egorenkova, G., "Vechnoe vremia." *Moskva,* no. 8 (1988), pp. 182-95.

Eliashevich, A "Gorod i gorozhane." *Zvezda,* no. 12 (1983), pp. 170-85.

Eremina, S., Piskunov, V. "Vremia i mesto prozy I. Trifonova." *Voprosy literatury,* no. 5 (1982), pp. 34-65.

Ermolaev, G. "Proshloe i nastoiashchee v 'Starike' I. Trifonova." *Russian Language Journal,* 37, no. 128 (1983), pp. 131-46.

Feldman, D. "Oshibka avtora ili oshibka geroia?" *Literaturnaia ucheba,* no. 6 (1987), pp. 169-74.

Filatova, A. "Postigaia istoriiu," *Neva,* no. 12 (1978), pp. 169-77.

Finitskaia, Z. "Pod iarkim solntsem." *Oktiabr',* no. 12 (1960), pp. 212-14.

Fink, L. "Zybkost' kharaktera ili zybkost' zamysla." *Literaturnaia gazeta,* 29 October 1975, p. 4.

Galanov, B. "Nachalo puti." *Znamia,* no. 1 (1951), pp. 171-74.

Geideko, V. "Liudi na rabote." *Zvezda,* no. 12 (1964), pp. 195-203.

Gladilshchikov, I. "Ne ischeznoveniie: Pamiat'." *Literaturnaia Rossiia,* 27 March 1987, p. 2.

Golovskoi, V. "Nravstvennye uroki trifonovskoi prozy." *Russian Language Journal,* 37, no. 128 (1983), 147-64.

Grinberg, I. "Perekrestki i paralleli." *Oktiabr',* no. 12 (1974), pp. 189-204.

Gus, M. "Zhizn' i sushchestvovanie." *Znamia,* no. 8 (1972), pp. 211-26.

Gusev, L. "Usloviia vstrechi." *Literaturnaia gazeta,* 4 February 1970, p. 6.

_____. "Prostranstvo slova: Stilistika prozy V. Belova i I. Trifonova." *Pamiat' i stil'.* Moskva, 1981, pp. 324-33.

Hosking, G. "Yury Trifonov." *Beyond Socialist Realism: Soviet Fiction since Ivan Denisovich.* New York: Homes and Meier, 1980, pp. 180-95.

Hughes, A. "Bolshoi mir or zamknutyi mirok: Departure from Literary Convention in I. Trifonov's Recent Fiction." *Canadian Slavonic Papers,* 12, no. 4 (1980), 470-80.

Iakimenko, L. "O poetike sovremennogo romana." *Druzhba narodov,* no. 5 (1971), pp. 234-45.

_____. "Literaturnaia kritika i sovremennaia povest'." *Novyi mir,* no. 1 (1973), pp. 238-50.

Iaroslavtsev, I. "Talantlivaia prostota." *Literaturnaia Rossiia,* 26 June 1970, p. 18.

Igolchenko, I. I. "Nekotorye nabliudeniia nad leksikoi sovetskogo istoricheskogo romana." *Materialy III respublikanskoi konferentsii aspirantov vuzov Azerbaidzhana.* Baku, 1981, pp. 412-19.

Il'ina, N. "Iz rodoslovnoi russkoi revolutsii: O romane I. Trifonova 'Neterpenie'." *Neman,* no. 12 (1976), pp. 170-75.

Ivanova, N. *Proza Iuriia Trifonova.* Moskva: Sovetskii pisatel', 1984.

_____. "Ottsy i deti epokhi." *Voprosy literatury,* no. 11 (1987), pp. 50-83.

Ivanova, V. "Legko li byt'?" *Druzhba narodov,* no. 5 (1987), pp. 231-48.

Kardin, V. "Neotvratimost' vybora." *Druzhba narodov,* no. 3 (1973), pp. 246-59.

_____. "Proroki v svoem otechestve." *Druzhba narodov,* no. 8 (1974), pp. 267-71.

_____. "Vremena ne vybiraiut: Iz zametok o I. Trifonove." *Novyi mir,* no. 7 (1987), pp. 236-57.

Khmara, V. "Protivostoianie." *Literaturnaia gazeta,* 28 June 1978, p. 5.

Klado, N. "Prokrustovo lozhe byta." *Literaturnaia gazeta*, 2 May 1976, p. 4.

Kolesnikoff, N. "Jurij Trifonov as Novella Writer." *Russian Language Journal*, 34, no. 118 (1980), pp, 137-43.

_____. "Trifonov's Time and Place: Compositional and Narrative Structure." *Russian Language Journal*, 41, no. 140 (1988), pp. 165-75.

Kozhinov, V. "Problema avtora i put' pisatelia: Na materiale dvukh povestei Iuriia Trifonova." *Kontekst* (1977), pp. 23-47.

Kramov, I. "Sud'ba i vremia." *Novyi mir*, no. 3 (1967), pp. 252-54.

Kutmina, O. "Vnutrennii monolog v povesti Iuriia Trifonova 'Drugaia zhizn': Nekotorye aspekty." *Problemy psikhologizma v khudozhestvennoi literature. Sbornik statei.* Tomsk, 1980, pp. 44-49.

Kuznetsov, F. "Nastuplenie novoi nravstvennosti." *Voprosy literatury*, no. 2 (1964), pp. 3-26.

_____. "Dukhovnye tsennosti: Mify i deistvitel'nost'." *Novyi mir*, no. 1 (1974), pp. 211-31.

_____. "Byt' chelovekom: O nekotorykh nravstvennykh problemakh sovremennoi prozy." *Oktiabr'*, no. 2 (1975), pp. 193-203.

Kuznetsova, N. "I komissary v pyl'nykh shlemakh." *Kontinent*, no. 53 (1987), pp. 391-96.

Lanshchikov, A. "Geroi i vremia." *Don*, no. 11 (1973), pp. 169-78.

Latynina, A. "Oskolok gologramy." *Literaturnaia gazeta*, 18 February 1987, p. 7.

Lazarev, L. "Bez egzotiki." *Druzhba narodov*, no. 6 (1959), pp. 227-29.

Lebedev, A. "Neterpimost'." *Vybor*, Moskva, 1980, pp. 193-246.

Leiderman, N. "Potentsial zhanra." *Sever*, no. 3 (1978), pp. 101-9.

Leitner, A. "Die verlorene und wiedergefundene Zeit in Jurij Trifonovs Roman 'Dom na nabereznoi'." *Slavisticna Revija*, 30, no. 4 (1982), 573-87.

Lemkhin, M. "Zheliabov, Nechaev, Karlos i drugie." *Kontinent*, no. 49 (1986), pp. 359-68.

Levin, L. "Vosem' stranits ot ruki." *Voprosy literatury*, no. 3 (1988), pp. 183-98.

Levina, L. "Siuzhetno-kompozitsionnye sredstva vyrazheniia soderzhaniia v povesti I. Trifonova 'Obmen'." *Sbornik nauchnykh trudov Tashkentskogo universiteta*, no. 571 (1978), pp. 40-55.

Lourie, R. "Tales of a Soviet Chekhov." *New York Times Book Review*, 18 March 1984, p. 7.

Lozhechko, A. "Povest' o studentakh." *Oktiabr'*, no. 1 (1951), pp. 185-88.

Lukianin, V. "Praktichnye liudi: Tema razoblacheniia meshchanstva v sovremennoi proze." *Ural*, no. 7 (1972), pp. 134-39.

Lur'e, A. "Uroki zhizni i tvorchestva." *Neva*, no. 4 (1978), pp. 179-81.

L'vov, S. "Povest' o sovremennykh studentakh." *Vydaiushchiesia proizvedeniia sovetskoi literatury 1950 goda: Sbornik statei.* Moskva: Sovetskii pisatel', 1952, p. 266-78.

Maegd-Soep, C. "The Theme of *byt* in the Stories of I. Trifonov." *Russian Literature and Criticism: Selected Papers from the Second World Congress On Soviet and European Studies.* Ed. E. Brystol. Berkeley: Berkeley Slavic Specialties, 1982, pp. 49-62.

Mai, B. "Die Suche nach dem 'anderen Leben' in den Werken Jurij Trifonovs." *Zeitschrift für Slavistik*, 27, no. 4 (1981), pp. 611-18.

_____. "Problembewusstsein im sozialistischen Alltag: zum Werk Jurij Trifonovs." *Wissenschaftliche Zeitschrift der Ernst Moritz Arndt—Universität Greifswald: Gesellschaftswissenschaftliche Reihe*, 35, 1-2 (1986), p. 85.

McLaughlin, S. "Jurij Trifonov's 'House on the Embankment': Narration and Meaning." *Slavic and East European Journal*, 26, no. 4 (1982), pp. 419-33.

_____. "Iurii Trifonov's *Dom na naberezhnoi* and Dostoevskii's *Prestuplenie i nakazanie.*" *Canadian Slavonic Papers*, 25, no. 2 (1983), pp. 275-83.

_____. "Antipov's *Nikiforov Syndrome:* The Embedded Novel in Trifonov's Time and

Place." *Slavic and East European Journal*, 32, no. 2 (1988), pp. 237-50.

Mikhailova, L. "Geroi otkrytykh gorizontov." *Literaturnaia gazeta*, 27 July 1963.

Murikov, G. "Pamiat." *Zvezda*, no. 12 (1987), pp. 166-76.

Naumova, N. "Sviaz' vremen." *Zvezda*, no. 6 (1976), pp. 195-202.

Neuhauser, R. "Die zeitgenössische russische Novelle am Beispiel von Jurij Trifonovs 'Dolgoe proscanie'." *Slavisticna Revija*, 30, no. 4 (1982), pp. 561-72.

————. "Trifonov: Langer Abschied." *Die russische Novelle*. Ed. B. Zelinsky. Düsseldorf: Bagel, 1982, pp. 252-63.

Nikol'skaia, T. Review of *Rasskazy i povesti*. *Zvezda*, no. 2 (1972), pp. 215-16.

Obozrevatel', "Chuvstvo puti." *Literaturnaia Rossiia*, 13 February 1987, p. 5.

Oklianskii, I. "Schastlivye neudachniki Iuriia Trifonova." *Literaturnoe obozrenie*, 11 November 1985, pp. 109-112.

————. *Iurii Trifonov: Portret—Vospominanie*. Moskva: Literaturnaia Rossiia, 1987.

Orekhova, N. "Vybrat' pozitsiiu." *Neva*, no. 10 (1979), pp. 195-96.

Oskotskii, V. "Nravstvennye uroki Narodnoi Voli." *Literaturnoe obozrenie*, no. 1 (1973), pp. 55-60.

————. "Roman i istoriia." *Voprosy literatury*, no. 8 (1973), pp. 3-45.

Ozerov, V. "Literaturno-khudozhestvennaia kritika i sovremennost'." *Voprosy literatury*, no. 4 (1972), pp. 3-39.

Paleeva, N. "Sviaz' vremen." *Molodaia gvardiia*, no. 9 (1979), pp. 281-91.

Pankin, B. "Po krugu ili po spirali." *Druzhba narodov*, no. 5 (1977), pp. 238-53.

Pankov, A. "Zaboty zhizni i puti literatury." *Druzhba narodov*, no. 10 (1985), pp. 217-29.

Parkhomenko, M. "Etika budushchego." *Druzhba narodov*, no. 4 (1974), pp. 236-46.

————. "Masshtabom nashei zhizni." *Voprosy literatury*, no. 6 (1976), pp. 50-79.

Patera, T. *Obzor tvorchestva i analiz moskovskikh povestei Iuriia Trifonova*. Ann Arbor: Ardis, 1983.

Perelygina, M. D. "Osobennosti zhanra i siuzhetno-kompozitsionnye struktury sovremennoi istoriko-biograficheskoi povesti o narodovol'tsakh." *Nauchnye trudy Kuibyshevskogo pedagogicheskogo instituta*, 227 (1979), 80-94.

Pertsovskii, V. "Proza vmeshyvaetsia v spor." *Voprosy literatury*, no. 10 (1971), pp. 27-48.

————. "Ispytanie bytom." *Novyi mir*, no. 11 (1974), pp. 236-51.

————. "Pokoriaias' techeniiu." *Voprosy literatury*, no. 4 (1979), pp. 3-35.

————. "Avtorskaia pozitsiia v literature i kritike." *Voprosy literatury*, no. 7 (1981), pp. 66-105.

Plekhanova, I. "Osobennosti siuzhetoslozheniia v tvorchestve V. Shukshina, I. Trifonova, V. Rasputina." *Russkaia literatura*, no. 4 (1980), pp. 71-88.

————. "Priroda nravstvennogo soznaniia v traktovke V. Shukshina, I. Trifonova, V. Rasputina." *Sibir'*, no. 5 (1980), pp. 82-92.

Plotkin, L. "Dorogi padeniia i progressa." *Zvezda*, no. 10 (1971), pp. 202-10.

Proffer, E. "Introduction." Y. Trifonov. *The Long Goodbye*. New York: Harper and Row, 1978, pp. 9-16.

Pu, V. "Ispytanie pustynei." *Ashkhabad*, no. 1 (1980), pp. 92-94.

Pukhov, I. "Vroven' s vekom." *Oktiabr'*, no. 6 (1971), pp. 191-208.

Ravich, N. "Podvig A. Zheliabova." *Literaturnaia gazeta*, 26 Sept. 1973, p. 5.

Reissner, E. "Auf der Suche nach der verlorenen Wahrheit: Jurij Trifonovs jungster Roman *Der Alte*." *Osteuropa*, 29 (1979), 99-109.

Reskov, B. "O smysle i krasote zhizni." *Zvezda Vostoka*, no. 6 (1965), pp. 144-46.

Riabova, L. "Sposoby sozdaniia rechi personazhei: Na materiale proizvedenii Zalygina, Rasputina, Trifonova, Shukshina." Diss. Saratovskii gosudarstvennyi universitet. Saratov, 1981.

Rogova, G. "Itogi i razdum'ia." *Pod'em*, no. 11 (1982), pp. 135-38.

Rosliakov, V. "Utolennaia zhazhda." *Moskva*, no. 10 (1963), pp. 204-6.

Rybal'chenko, T. "Zhanrovaia struktura i khudozhestvennaia ideia: Povest' I. Trifonova 'Predvaritel'nye itogi'. *Problemy metoda i zhanra.* Tomsk, 1977, pp. 98-105.

_____. "Povest' i rasskaz v sovremennom literaturnom protsesse." Diss. Tomskii gosudarstvennyi universitet. Tomsk, 1978.

Sadin, E. "Kochka zreniia." *Ashkhabad*, 1 (1959), pp. 262-65.

Sakharov, V. "Flamandskoi shkoly pestryi master." *Nash sovremennik*, no. 5 (1974), pp. 188-91.

_____. "Vospominatel'naia proza, poteri i obreteniia: Zametki o povestiakh I. Trifonova." *Obnovliaiushchiisia mir: Zametki o tekuchei literature.* Moskva: Sovremennik, 1980, pp. 173-96.

Sappak, V. "Zamysel obiazyvaet." *Teatr*, no. 3 (1954), pp. 93-102.

Satretdinova, R. "Natsional'noe i internatsional'noe v kharaktere turkmena v proizvedeniiakh russkikh pisatelei: Na primere romana I. Trifonova 'Utolenie zhazhdy'." *Izvestiia Akademii nauk Turkmenskoi SSR*, no. 5 (1981), pp. 48-53.

_____. "Obrazy rozhdennye real'nost'iu: Turkmenskaia tema v tvorchestve pisatelia I. Trifonova." *Ashkhabad*, no. 5 (1981), pp. 78-82.

_____. *Turkmenistan v tvorchestve I. V. Trifonova.* Ashkhabad, 1984.

Savateev, V. "Molodost' dushi." *Nash sovremennik*, no. 7 (1973), pp. 167-73.

_____. "Geroi podlinnye i mnimye." *Literaturnaia Rossiia*, 13 February 1976, pp. 14-15.

Schulte, B. "Jurij Trifonovs 'Der Tausch' und Valentin Rasputins 'Geld für Maria'." *Ein Beitrag zum Gattungsverständnis von Povest' und Rasskaz.* Göttingen: Vandenhoeck und Ruprecht, 1985.

Shenfel'd, I. "I. Trifonov—pisatel' chastichnoi pravdy." *Grani*, no. 121 (1981), pp. 112-18.

Shklovskii, E. "Razrushenie doma." *Literaturnoe obozrenie*, no. 7 (1987), pp. 46-48.

_____. "Samoe glavnoe." *Literaturnoe obozrenie*, no. 11 (1987), pp. 25-34.

Shneidman, N. "Iurii Trifonov and the Ethics of Contemporary City Life." *Canadian Slavonic Papers*, 19, no. 3 (1977), pp. 335-51.

_____. "Iurii Trifonov: City Prose." *Soviet Literature in the 1970's: Artistic Diversity and Ideological Conformity.* Toronto: University of Toronto Press, 1979, pp. 88-105.

_____. "The New Dimensions of Time and Place in Iurii Trifonov's Prose of the 1980's." *Canadian Slavonic Papers*, 27, no. 2 (1985), 188-95.

Shtokman, I. "Volny moria zhiteiskogo." *Iunost'*, no. 6 (1972), p. 70.

Shtut, S. "Rassuzhdeniia i opisaniia." *Voprosy literatury*, no. 10 (1975), pp. 38-72.

_____. "I slovo est' delo." *Literaturnaia gazeta*, 12 June 1978, p. 4.

Shugaev, V. "Moskovskii roman ili muzhestvo pisatelia." *Literaturnaia Rossiia*, 24 April 1987, p. 5.

Sinel'nikov, M. "Ispytanie povsednevnost'iu: nekotorye itogi." *Voprosy literatury*, no. 2 (1972), pp. 46-62.

_____. "Poznat' cheloveka, poznat' vremia." *Voprosy literatury*, no 9 (1979), pp. 26-52.

Skorino, L. "Skhema i skhima." *Znamia*, no. 2 (1964), pp. 237-43.

Smirnov, S. "Sovremennyi istoriko-revolutsionnyi roman: Voprosy poetiki zhanra." Diss. Tomskii gosudarstvennyi universitet. Tomsk, 1979.

_____. "Sovremennost' istorii." *Sibir'*, no. 2 (1981), pp. 66-70.

Sokolov, V. "Rasshcheplenie obydennost'iu." *Voprosy literatury*, no. 2 (1972), pp. 31-45.

Solodar', Ts. "Priznanie v liubvi." *Literaturnaia gazeta*, 15 October 1965, p. 23.

Solov'ev, V. "O liubvi i ne tol'ko o liubvi." *Literaturnoe obozrenie*, no. 2 (1976), pp. 38-40.

Sozonova, I. "Vnutri kruga." *Literaturnoe obozrenie*, no. 5 (1976), pp. 53-56.

Ssachno, H. "Moskauer Geschichten: Zu den Romanen von Jurij Trifonov." *Schweizer Rundschau: Zeitschrift für Geistesleben, Kultur, Reisen*, no. 57 (1977), pp. 399-404.

Stepanenko, E. "Tainstvo tvorchestva." *Sever*, no. 2 (1985), pp. 110-16.

Surovtsev, I. "O povestiakh 'etazherkakh' i o dvizhenii po 'vertikali'." *Zvezda*, no. 2 (1971), pp. 191-201.

_____. "Nepriiatie meshchanstva." *Zvezda*, no. 7 (1972), pp. 198-213.

_____. "Sotsial'nyi obraz zhizni i literatury." *Literaturnaia gazeta*, 9 June 1976, p. 2.

Svetov, F. Review of *Utolenie zhazhdy*. *Novyi mir*, no. 11 (1963), pp. 235-40.

Svobodin, A. "Liudi svoei sud'by." *Literatura i sovremennost'*, no. 13 (1975), pp. 368-73.

Talanova, O. "Khudozhestvennaia manera I. Trifonova." *Problemy poetiki*. Alma-Ata: Kazakhskii gosudarstvennyi universitet, 1980, pp. 101-12.

Tereklian, D. "Preodoleniia." *Druzhba narodov*, no. 4 (1971), pp. 252-64.

Terekopian, L. "Poznanie kharaktera." *Druzhba narodov*, no. 10 (1969), pp. 234-46.

Tikhovov, I. "Delo kotoromu ty sluzhish'." *Oktiabr'*, no. 1 (1964), pp. 212-15.

Tiul'pinov, N. "Otblesk drugoi zhizni." *Zvezda*, no. 2 (1976), pp. 216-18.

Trifonova-Miroshnichenko, O. "Sopriazhenie istorii s sovremennost'iu." *Voprosy literatury*, no. 7 (1987), pp. 170-85.

Turkov, A. "Ne boias' povtorit'sia." *Znamia*, no. 5 (1987), pp. 232-34.

Tvardovskaia, V. "Po povodu publikatsii pisem Iuriia Trifonova." *Voprosy literatury*, no. 2 (1988), pp. 192-95.

Updike, J. "Czarist Shadows, Soviet Lilacs." *The New Yorker*, 11 Sept. 1978, pp. 153-58.

Woll, J. "Trifonov's *Starik:* The Truth of the Past." *Russian Literature Triquarterly*, no. 19 (1986), pp. 243-60.

Zolotonosov, M. "Muzyka vo l'du." *Ural*, no. 3 (1988), pp. 167-68.

Zolotusskii, I. "Vozvyshchaiushchee slovo." *Literaturnoe obozrenie*, no. 6 (1988), pp. 23-32.

INDEX